MY PATH LEADS TO TIBET

Sabriye lost her sight at the age of twelve, and had promised herself not to allow her blindness to turn her into an invalid. When she learned that, in Tibet, many blind children were shunned by society, abandoned and left to their own devices, she decided to journey there to help them . . . She devised a Tibetan Braille alphabet and opened the first school for the blind in Lhasa. That school is now an institution for visually impaired people of all ages. Sabriye shares the inspiring story of how she shone an unlikely light in a dark place.

SABRIYE TENBERKEN

MY PATH
LEADS TO TIBET

The Inspiring Story of How
One Young Blind Woman Brought Hope
to the Blind Children of Tibet

Complete and Unabridged

ULVERSCROFT
Leicester

First published in the United States
Arcade Publishing, Inc.
New York

First Large Print Edition
published 2007
by arrangement with
Arcade Publishing, Inc.
New York

Photography courtesy of Paul Kronenberg

British Library CIP Data

Tenberken, Sabriye, *1970 –*
  My path leads to Tibet.—Large print ed.—
  Ulverscroft large print series: non-fiction
  1. Blind children—Education—China—Tibet
  2. Blind children—Rehabilitation—China—Tibet
  3. Blind children—Services for—China—Tibet
  4. Large type books
  I. Title
  362.4′1′09515

  ISBN 978–1–84617–941–9

Published by
F. A. Thorpe (Publishing)
Anstey, Leicestershire

Set by Words & Graphics Ltd.
Anstey, Leicestershire
Printed and bound in Great Britain by
T. J. International Ltd., Padstow, Cornwall

This book is printed on acid-free paper

In memory of Frans van Bennekom
Valiant warrior, founder of
Target for Eyes

Acknowledgments

I would like to thank the Tibetologist Thierry Dodin for his advice and counsel.

The names of certain people who appear in this book have been changed to protect their identity.

Publisher's Note

The author has chosen to refer to people who can see — as opposed to the blind — as 'sighted', as in the terms 'sighted children' or 'sighted people'. Although that usage may at first strike the reader as awkward or a bit strange, it seemed to us that it was more direct and clear than such descriptive phrases as 'people who can see' or 'those with normal eyesight'.

1

'Kelsang Meto! Kelsang Meto!'

The cries came from below. I urged my horse forward. Calm and confident, he placed his hooves gingerly on the stony slope. There wasn't a right way to go, and from time to time the horse stopped, as if to weigh which boulder promised the safest step.

'Kelsang Meto! Come back!' The voices, full of fear, sounded as if they came from far away.

But I didn't want to turn back now. I knew I mustn't interrupt the horse's concentration, and the way back might be even more dangerous. Rocks tumbled toward us, and now and then the horse made a daring leap to avoid them. He was a small native mountain-bred horse, a past master in the art of climbing.

I had been warned: this stallion was aggressive and often tried to get rid of his rider by bucking. But I also bucked at times, so I resolved to put myself in the care of this 'devil.' And now I was glad I had, because the horse, called Nagpo, 'the black one,' by his owner, was calm and highly focused. As a child I had learned to deal with horses that were reputedly difficult and temperamental. But I had also learned that they were often sensitive and intelligent animals, and I soon knew that I could trust them without hesitation.

'Kelsang Meto!' another cry echoed from below. 'There's a storm brewing. We can't go over the pass!'

'We have to!' I called back. 'There's a village on the other side. I'm sure we'll find shelter there!'

A farmer had warned us that we were in for a heavy storm: we should try to reach the next village as quickly as possible. On this side of the pass all we would find would be a few tufts of grass between heaps of boulders to camp on, but nothing that would offer us any real protection during the night.

Nagpo stopped briefly to listen to our calls. After my subdued 'Tschua!' he moved forward. I'd spent five days on the back of this horse, and in the meantime we had agreed on a language of our own. I didn't need to use a crop or a whip; even pulling the reins or squeezing my thighs was no longer necessary. All I had to do was give concise orders and shift my weight slightly.

Suddenly the wind rose, whistled in our ears, and tore at our luggage, which was strapped behind me on the saddle. Its velocity was increasing by the minute, and I knew the storm was not far behind. Luckily, the gusts weren't dangerous; coming from the rear, they merely pressed us more tightly against the mountain.

Before long, I heard the panting of the others, who had decided after all to risk crossing the pass. They dismounted and were walking beside their mounts, leading them by the reins. I'd rather rely on my horse, letting the reins hang loose, concentrating entirely on keeping Nagpo calm.

But we made it. My horse stood on the mountain peak, bathed in sweat and snorting heavily. The storm did its best to push us over to the other side of the mountain. I dismounted, stood beside Nagpo to protect myself from the wind, and waited for the others, who were not far behind. I was convinced that the worst was behind us, and all of a sudden I realized that the tension had completely worn me out. What I didn't know was that what I had gone through so far was nothing compared to the real inferno that lay ahead.

Once everyone had reached the peak, out of breath and cursing loudly, we moved warily on. The first stretch of path led along a tight ridge. I went first with Nagpo, praying that on the other side we would find a passable road. My stallion had a stronger will, was more firm than the other horses, so was therefore the leader. He also seemed to have an extraordinary intuition about where best to step. He chose his route with utter care, testing it with his hooves. The earth slid under his steps, stones fell into the yawning precipice. There really wasn't any right way to go.

Nagpo hesitated for a moment, then set forth: he jumped from one boulder to another, a highly dangerous leap, as my travel companions later reported, that crossed a wide and incredibly deep crevice. During the jump, my left stirrup broke loose, and after a frightfully long few seconds, I heard it clang quietly, far, far below on the rocky floor.

I became conscious of my fear of heights, and for an instant I was gripped by a sudden cold horror. But I quickly pulled myself together. I didn't have time to think of what might have happened if I had not been able to stay in the saddle. We moved on briskly. From boulder to boulder, from jump to jump, deeper and deeper.

'Kelsang Meto!' The voices sounded distressed. The others came to a halt on the other side of the crevice.

On even ground — a small plateau of

rocks, I presumed — I brought Nagpo to a halt. 'I'll wait for you here,' I called out. 'Find another way!' I waited for a long time, far too long. Dark thoughts flashed through my mind. What if the storm, which now was howling around us, snatched them up and threw them into the precipice?

Many long minutes later I heard them approach from the other side. But I heard something else too, an ominous rumbling of thunder in the distance, fast approaching. 'Move on! Move on!' they called out to me, and with a quiet 'Tschua!' I set Nagpo in motion again.

The storm raged even more strongly. It pulled at my saddle strap, tore the hat from my head. I let it fly away. People here thought that it brought bad luck if you found a hat you had lost. That was the last thing I needed right now. What was important was focusing on the immediate problem: the wild storm. The thunder sounded as if all the gods in heaven were at war. The air was full of sand and fine dust that sifted into my eyes. I pulled a bandanna over my eyes; the fact was, I didn't need them. I needed my ears, I needed my mouth to keep the horse's spirits up with reassuring utterances, and I needed my sense of balance to stay securely on the wooden saddle, especially now that the cinch was coming loose. The only thing that mattered was the movement beneath me, the horse's every step and jump.

'Kelsang Meto!' someone called from behind me. 'More to the right! The precipice is on the left!'

Horses like to follow a path. And I was aware that my left foot was dangling stirrupless over the void. But I could not and would not influence the horse anymore. I simply had to rely on the fact that he knew what he was doing.

Nagpo reared, hearing the thunder hard upon us. I heard a loud crash, tumbling rocks, horses neighing in panic, and then a cry that shook my concentration. What was that? It sounded as if a boulder had fallen into the precipice, dragging someone with it. In my imagination I saw a shattered body at the bottom of the ravine. The thought flashed through my mind that it was I who had forced them to follow me over the pass. They hadn't wanted to let me go alone. And it would be my fault if something terrible had happened.

I tried to turn Nagpo around on the narrow path, but he resisted — rightly so, I thought. What should I do? Was it fair to just sit here and wait? I tried to turn Nagpo one more time, but he started bucking: all he wanted was to continue his downward journey. To keep the now overly skittish horse still, I dismounted. A thunderclap, the loudest yet, rattled the night, and it started to pour. The rainwater fell on me in powerful cold sheets, seeping into my clothes, until soon I was drenched to the bone. Suddenly I heard the sound of hooves quickly approaching from above. 'What happened?' I called out into the darkness.

I heard a voice, but the pouring rain and whistling wind swallowed the words. Only when they got closer did I hear what they had said: 'Move on, move on! Nothing has happened, just a small fall!'

I climbed back onto the saddle and, followed by the clattering hooves of the horses and the stumbling boots of the riders, I urged Nagpo farther down. We passed a small outcrop, and I noticed that the path under his hooves was gradually becoming even and sandy.

★   ★   ★

We and our horses had found refuge under the jutting roof of a barn, the horses trembling from the tension and cold. We didn't have long to wait: minutes after we arrived, an angry farmer had emerged from his house and shooed us all away — as if we were thieves in the night — back into the rain. We tried again at a neighboring hut, but this time they set the dogs on us. Evidently we didn't look particularly appealing.

At last an old farmer's wife opened a window and listened to what we had to say, Dolma stood in front of her, pointed at our small caravan, and began her lecture. She described the long and arduous path over the high pass, pointed out our sopping wet clothes and her own leg, which she had injured when she fell.

'Ozi-ah!' murmured the farmer's wife, seemingly full of compassion. Nonetheless, she didn't offer us her hospitality.

To clearly illustrate our sorry state, Dolma hobbled up and down in front of the window, accompanying her movements with cries of pain. Apparently she was making some extremely funny faces, for suddenly the farmer's wife emitted a throaty laugh. Shortly thereafter, however, she must have thought the show too silly, or us too pitiful, for without further ado she pulled her head back into her cozy hut and slammed the window shut.

Completely discouraged, we stood there with our horses in the torrential rain. We begged Dolma to give us one more try. A couple of huts farther on, she called out into the darkness, 'Ohlohi!' Soon a couple of windows opened.

'All we need is a roof over our heads, perhaps a stable too!' Dolma cried out, and she really sounded miserable.

'Where do you come from?' the skeptical farmer wanted to know.

Dolma explained that we'd been traveling by horse for over a week, in order to tell blind people about a new form of writing for the blind. 'Kelsang Meto herself is blind!' she said, grabbing my sleeve and pushing me forward like an exhibit in front of the open window.

'*Huuu!* A foreigner!' the children called out excitedly as they stuck their heads out of the window.

'Kelsang Meto,' Dolma said, and now she was going full steam, 'Kelsang Meto came alone from the West all the way to Tibet, so she can teach blind people how to read and write!'

'*Nying dscheh!* How touching!' the farmers' wives murmured, and they clicked their tongues in sympathy. But nothing more.

Now Dolma lost her temper, her voice almost broken: 'If you don't take us in tonight, then it will be said that Tibetans aren't hospitable, that they let foreigners freeze to death on their doorstep!'

Finally her call to native pride seemed to have an effect. Slowly, a door was pushed open, and a friendly old man said to us, 'Please come in.'

2

'Passengers for flight CA 936 to Beijing are now boarding at Gate B.'

This was not the first time I had gone to China, nor was it the first time I had traveled alone. But that had not kept me from having been admonished and criticized relentlessly.

'Why in the world are you going on this foolish trip anyway?' asked Thierry, a doctoral student in Tibetan studies. 'In any case, my dear friend, you can't go by yourself. You'll need a man to squire you around. Wait until next semester, and I'll go with you to Lhasa.'

Then there was a fellow student who, upon hearing of my plan, burst out laughing. '*Alone and Blind in Tibet!* What a perfect title for a Hollywood production!'

Or my girlfriend's mother, who gravely and with obvious concern inquired whether my parents had given me permission to take this trip. At that point in my life I was twenty-six.

'What are you trying to prove, always doing things on your own?' my then boyfriend, Christopher, offered. 'Finish up your studies, we'll move in together, and I'll go with you.'

Some time back, the two of us had gone to

China, but after a month he had returned to Germany, leaving me alone to explore a tiny segment of that immense country. At first I had been terribly apprehensive, not at all sure I would be able to navigate without the help of a seeing companion. But as I learned to trust fate and roll with the punches, things seemed to fall into place, and I continued the trip on my own.

Back in Germany, after living for a fair amount of time without any specific plans or schedules, I found that I sorely missed my short-lived independence. My friends, my professors, everyone around me — all self-appointed experts on what was best for me — seemed to focus solely on the negative aspects, seemingly intent on knocking my project and putting down my planned new trip. I found it both irritating and stifling.

Undeterred, I proceeded with my plans. This time it would be to fulfill my long-standing ambition: to found a school for blind children in Tibet.

'Dropping everything and leaving me behind just to satisfy your ego! Bravo!' my boyfriend lamented, thinking more of himself than of me, I felt.

I refused to feel guilty. 'Why don't you pack your bags, leave your job, and join me?' I challenged.

'Why don't you grow up?' chimed in Gerald, one of Christopher's close friends. 'You clearly haven't a clue, Sabriye, no notion of the future. What about security? Someday you'll understand what it means to have a family, your own house, to hold a steady job. When you get to be sixty, say, it'll be important for you to look back at what you've done with your life!'

This kind of moralizing drove me crazy, not to mention his logic. Was I supposed to stop living, stop enjoying life, stop *dreaming*, until I was *sixty*? At which point I could look back on what I *hadn't* done? Still, Gerald had touched on one sensitive point. What *was* I doing, really? Was the road I was proposing to follow really the right one? Wasn't pursuing my studies and landing a good job perhaps the more sensible thing to do? Also, was traveling alone to Tibet to try and better the life of blind children there — no doubt an absurdly idealistic plan — not a completely foolish endeavor after all? Didn't this project need large teams of experts, well-funded organizations, not to mention veteran travel agents to take charge of exotic foreign expeditions? What had possessed me to go it alone, without any real preparation? Was I being arrogant? To this day I don't know the answers to these questions. All I know is, in my heart I felt that what I was doing was right.

Strange as it may seem, whenever I'm about to take a leap into the unknown, I always have the same dream. I'm standing at the top of a sand dune, looking down at the sea. The sky is clear and blue, the sea flat and dark. The sun is bright, the beach is filled with people. Then all of a sudden, on the horizon a huge towering wall of water is moving slowly toward us in total silence. Everyone is running in my direction. The wall of water, growing ever more menacing by the second, blots out most of the sky. Instead of running away, I walk toward it. And the wall of water crashes over me. To my surprise, however, instead of being crushed by its mass, I am in my dream left feeling tremendously light, filled with new energy. And I know that from now on nothing will be impossible.

★ ★ ★

'Passengers for Flight CA 936 traveling to Beijing are now boarding at Gate B!'

'The second call, Sabriye. You'd better get a move on,' my parents urged.

I knew they had to be feeling a bit tense, but to their credit they didn't let any of their

14

anxiety show. Confident I would always be able to cope with, and come out on top of, any situation, they were at peace with my plans. In fact, my mother seemed to share my excitement. As a student, she too had left home and country behind to live in Turkey and study Islamic art, in Ankara. Often obliged to disguise herself as a man to avoid people raising an eyebrow, she had traveled through eastern Anatolia with a group of architectural students, visiting Seljukid mosques and writing reports.

'If you really want something badly enough,' she had always taught me, 'you'll end up getting it.'

'There's really nothing so extraordinary about this trip,' I managed to say as casually as I could, in a weak effort to reassure them — and no doubt myself as well. 'Besides, what makes me any different from other tourists?' I added unconvincingly.

The third boarding call rang out loud and clear. Feigning total calm, and hoping to hide the sudden excitement that had come over me, I checked my numerous pockets one last time, to make sure I had all my documents.

After giving my parents a last good-bye hug, I hopped onto one of those electric carts that had magically materialized to drive me through the interminable corridors of the

Frankfurt airport — a comfortable and amusing little diversion if it weren't for the fact that I can walk perfectly well and feel a bit silly being driven inside the airport.

'Where are you going?' the driver asked.

'Beijing,' I replied, 'then Tibet.'

'*Alone?*' I could hear disbelief in his voice.

I nodded, as if what I was doing was the most natural thing in the world. Truth to tell, I was beginning to get incredibly excited. And the man's surprise gave me an even greater kick. After escorting me through a number of passport controls, he again asked, 'How are you going to . . . how are you going to *cope?*'

'I haven't yet made any specific plans,' I answered. 'With me, something unexpected always happens. I like to keep my options open and trust to fate.'

'But who's going to help you? You'll be completely alone over there.'

'If I need help, I won't be alone. All I'll have to do is stand there in some crowded place, with my white cane visible. China is swarming with people, as you know. In less than ten minutes, I guarantee you, someone will come up to me and ask if I am in need of help.'

He fell silent, probably giving me a highly skeptical look.

'What's nice about my situation is that

wherever I go, I inevitably run into people who are intelligent, friendly, and open-minded. Anyone else wouldn't take the time or trouble to bother with a blind person, anyway.'

'Of course,' echoed the driver, marking the point that he of course belonged to the former — intelligent and friendly — type.

Just then, a whole group of frantic travelers — either lost in the immensity of the Frankfurt airport or late for their plane — materialized in front of our cart, blocking us.

'Stop! Stop! Blind transport! Let us by!' the driver shouted, loudly honking his horn, leaving me, of course, completely mortified. The passengers made way for us. I could only imagine their surprise, and inevitable compassion, at the sight of me sitting there alone with my white cane.

I hate that kind of situation. Back home, I'm constantly embarrassed in crowded buses whenever a well-meaning passenger admonishes another who is occupying a seat reserved for the handicapped, and asks that the seat be given to me. I've made it a habit to stand by the door so I can exit easily, without being pushed.

Once when I expressed my embarrassment at having been offered someone's seat, and insisted that I preferred to stand, I remember that person commenting, with considerable irritation, 'At least she should show a little gratitude when I offer her a helping hand!'

I am continually surprised that so many people cling to the cliché that blind people are totally vulnerable, the object of pity and compassion. Being patronized and made to feel like a little girl still upsets me today.

'Those poor blind people! You can't help but feel sorry for them! But the fact is, they can't take care of themselves' was a refrain I heard throughout my childhood, and it always provoked in me tears of rage and humiliation. But as time went on, I learned to accept all this with a modicum of humor.

We arrived at Gate B, and the driver stepped off to help me down. Appreciating his gallantry, I nonetheless made a point of jumping out on my own, letting him carry my bag to make him feel better.

'She's blind, and traveling alone. To *Tibet!* Please take good care of her!' I heard him whisper to the flight attendant.

★ ★ ★

The passenger in the seat next to me turned out to be a German flight engineer. For some reason, I found that reassuring. It wasn't clear what he could actually do if the plane developed a mechanical problem, but doubtless in the event of a strange event or an odd noise his cogent answers would help me understand and feel better, I thought.

The passenger on my other side was Chinese. He was absorbed in reading the *China Daily*, which I had heard him ask the stewardess for. After dinner, I decided it was time to try out my rudimentary Chinese on him.

'Excuse me, sir, do you live in Beijing?'

No answer.

'Er, do you have any children?'

Still no answer. Had he perhaps nodded? Or maybe he didn't want to admit to not having children?

'I don't have any children either,' I blurted out in an effort to put him at ease, adding that I was twenty-six and studying Central Asian history and geography at the University of Bonn. His continued silence was beginning to unnerve me. He must be shy, I decided. Or my Chinese was worse than I thought.

'Forgive my Chinese, I only recently started learning the language, and in fact I've been studying it only for a short while — '

Just then, the German engineer tapped me on the shoulder. 'Your Chinese neighbor,' he said, 'is fast asleep. He has earphones clapped to both ears. So don't take offense.'

* * *

Eleven hours later we landed in Beijing. It was noon, local time. The humid heat was a shocking contrast to Germany's cold, dry weather. The sun seemed so intense I actually had trouble breathing.

My friendly German engineer took me by the arm and escorted me over to the passport window, where he wished me success. 'I'm sure I'll be reading about you in the press,' he said.

'Blind Student Disappears Somewhere in China' is more the headline I imagined.

* * *

So here I was, in China. Alone. I wasn't afraid. Just a bit nervous. Not much different from the way I used to feel before exams.

I needed to collect my luggage. Practicing what I had declared with great assurance to the cart driver in Frankfurt, I planted myself with my cane in the middle of the airport and waited. I heard the clickety-click of high heels and the heavier sound of solid shoes passing in front of me; the sound of children shouting; fragments of Chinese, German, and English. But no one stopped to offer a helping hand. Undeterred, I followed the flow of humans a bit farther and stopped at a point where I heard someone asking an employee — probably behind a window — where he could find a bank. Ah, thought I, the same employee will surely lead me to the baggage claim.

'Over there! Can't you see the sign!' was her gruff answer through her window.

'I can't see! Can someone please help me?' I said, lifting my cane for one and all to see. Still to no avail.

I later learned that 'I can't see' and 'I can't read' sound very much alike in Chinese. 'If you can't read Chinese, read the sign in English over there!' she offered through the window.

By now a crowd of people had formed. 'This foreign lady is blind,' one man shouted. 'She needs someone to take her over to the baggage claim!' Thanks to him, someone finally did materialize, escorted me to the baggage claim, and pulled my luggage off the carrousel. Now that I had it, my next job was to locate the taxi stand. To my surprise, I was able to find it without too much trouble.

Not bad for my first hour in China, I congratulated myself. I had managed to retrieve my luggage, find a taxi, even negotiate the fee in Chinese! Here I was seated in a Beijing taxi, on my way to my hotel in the center of the city — a small victory, but victory nonetheless.

3

Sixteen hours later I woke up from a sound sleep — completely famished.

The next order of the day was finding a restaurant. In my previous experience in China, finding a place to eat was always relatively simple. All you need to do is follow your nose, in virtually any street. A fragrant aroma almost always leads you to some wonderful eatery. Just to make sure, however, I usually stop a passerby to double-check, and he or she usually confirms that my sense of smell has not betrayed me. Except once, when two teenagers broke into a loud giggle and quickly led me to the building next door. Ever since, I have wondered what that first place might have been.

Once you're inside a restaurant, the next job is finding an available seat. I know that tourists with normal eyesight generally go straight to the kitchen and point to various dishes. For someone like me, however, it's a whole other problem. Finding a seat was fairly easy: after I'd been standing for a few minutes at the restaurant entrance, along with the Chinese customers, the waiter finally led me to the appropriate table. Dutifully, I followed him, inevitably — and intentionally — stumbling against some chairs or tables along the way to let him know I'm blind.

Now came time to order — chapter 8 of my braille Chinese studybook. Because it consists of four huge, heavy folders, however, each 150 pages long, I had left it at home.

Totally lost, I ordered rice and soup.

'Was that really all you wanted?' asked the waiter, clearly disappointed.

I hadn't eaten for a full day, and the fact was, I would definitely have welcomed some more hearty food.

'Can you suggest something?' I asked.

Mistake number one.

He proceeded to rattle off some forty dishes, all named for flowers and other mysterious things, leaving me even more lost.

'Could you please choose for me?'

Mistake number two.

Within minutes platters appeared, followed by bowl after bowl of aromatic delicacies: pork in a honey sauce, crab in paprika, chicken with almonds and ginger, mushrooms in a spicy sauce, and an array of vegetables whose names I still do not know.

A feast for at least four!

Not yet proficient with chopsticks, I ended up leaving most of the food untouched. I had just paid a fortune for this no doubt delicious meal, but I was still hungry.

* * *

My next few days were spent in Beijing, waiting to pursue my journey on to Chengdu. I took the opportunity to turn those days into a kind of personal apprenticeship. Having come from a country where maternal instinct and the Good Samaritan syndrome appear the minute people see the tip of a blind person's cane, I was unprepared for the Chinese approach to the blind. Back home, every time I stand at a pedestrian crossing there is always a passerby with a civic sense to take my arm and, without asking, help me cross the street.

Not so in Beijing. First of all, there are very few pedestrian crossings and traffic lights. Secondly, unlike westerners, most Chinese don't know what a white cane means.

'You won't need this here,' an old woman told me one day on a Beijing street. 'Here there are buses, trams, and taxis everywhere.' I realized she had mistaken my white cane for a walking stick. The same thing happened in Tibet, where I was often asked if I was a shepherd, or whether the stick was something I used for skiing.

I had gotten used to such remarks. Even back home, someone once asked me, 'Is that for detecting mines?'

* * *

'Have you been blind since birth?' asked a six-year-old girl seated next to me in the plane to Chengdu.

'Carrie!' scolded her English mother, 'one doesn't ask such a question!'

On the contrary, her question had cleared the air. Sweeping the mother's embarrassment aside, I replied, 'My parents noticed I had eye problems when I was very little. But in those days, I could still see. Until I was twelve I could make out faces and see landscapes . . . I could also see colors, and I painted quite a lot.'

Even today, colors continue to play an important role in my life. Way back, on the advice of the ophthalmologist, my parents helped me practice distinguishing colors for as long as possible, which turned out to be very precious for me later on. It wasn't long before it became impossible for me to make out shapes or forms any longer, and I began relying on colors to orient myself. On my bike, I used the green lines on the road, or the darker lines of the sidewalk, to guide me. But colors are also an important mnemonic device for me. As far back as I can remember, numbers and words have instantly triggered colors in me. Take the number 4, for example: it represents the color gold. Five is light green. Nine is vermilion. Telephone numbers, mathematical equations, or any kind of formulas are easier for me to remember, thanks to my old habit of putting colors to numbers. Days of the week as well as months have their colors, too. I have them arranged in geometric formations, in circular sectors, a little like a pie. When I need to recall on which day a particular event happened, the first thing that pops up on my inner screen is the day's color, then its position in the pie. When I was little and explained my system to people, I was made to feel I was crazy. But this method served me well, and proved immensely useful throughout my school years.

'And what do you see today?' asked Carrie.

'An ophthalmologist would tell you that I see nothing. But in my imagination, and in my dreams, I see plenty of things. Land-scapes, colors, even faces.'

'Aren't you sad not to see?'

No one had ever asked me that question before. I took some time before answering: 'When I was very little, I cried a lot. It was mostly about being misunderstood. Either other people thought I could see normally and didn't understand why I didn't react the way they expected, or they judged me a hopeless case because I was blind. Even more galling, they would also always speak to me slowly and very loudly, as if the problem was with my brain, not my eyes. And when they saw me with someone they didn't know, or with my parents, they would simply address themselves directly to them, not to me — Would *she* like a piece of candy? Or, Do these shoes fit *her* properly?'

'But you are only blind, not deaf! And you certainly have no trouble expressing yourself!' said Carrie.

28

4

When I look back on my stay in Chengdu, the first thing that comes to mind is the extreme heat and humidity. So perpetually overcast was the region that the locals used to say that whenever a ray of sun manages to pierce the clouds, the dogs all start barking. Nonetheless I found Chengdu rather pleasant. People seemed nicer and less frenetic than in Beijing. I enjoyed walking with students through the campus of Chengdu University. Overcoming my fears, I even ventured through traffic, making my way carefully through the narrow market streets. I also often lingered on public squares or small bridges, pausing to take in the city's noises and smells. During one of my walks, I sensed the presence of several people around me — all strangely silent. Not hearing the sound of any clicking cameras, I concluded they weren't tourists. I became increasingly uncomfortable, and opted to try a joke in the hope of loosening things up.

'Why are you staring at me?' I finally asked. 'I'm not a panda, after all!' Both Chinese and foreign tourists make a point of going out of their way to view that endangered species in zoos and research centers in the Sichuan province. My audience, however, apparently didn't appreciate my comparison and remained standing around me in silence.

'We know you're not a panda,' someone answered, showing no sign of humor, 'but you are a foreigner!'

Chinese and westerners don't always share the same sense of humor. On another occasion, during the rainy season, I was taking a walk along a flooded road, unsuccessfully avoiding the puddles, soaked up to my knees, when out of the blue a man asked me, 'Why don't you go around the puddles?'

'Because I love water, and really enjoy swimming,' I answered his stupid question, wishing he had the same amount of mud and water in his shoes as I had. The irony having escaped him entirely, he went on, 'But really, if you want to swim, there's a pool not far from here.'

In Chengdu I had gotten to know a group of Chinese artists who often took me along with them to their local watering hole in the center of town. It was called the Little Bar, and reminded me of my student bars back home. They described to me in detail the walls, which they had decorated with their art slogans and posters, and the tables lighted by guttering candles. On a small elevated stage, various bands performed each night, while at the long bar students and budding artists drank beer while debating the philosophy of Marx and Engel, and art in general. Tang Lei, the owner of the bar, who had worked in Bonn and spoke German fluently, was busy pouring cocktails and beer.

'Do you know you're something of a celebrity here?' she said. 'Everyone's talking about the blind European girl who's going to travel on horseback throughout our country, to help blind Tibetans.' She poured me a cool beer. 'Tonight it's on me. You're our guest. For what you're doing for our people.'

'Thank you,' I answered, feeling very little like a celebrity. Up to now, I had made literally no progress at all toward that lofty goal. Part of the problem was that I had been unable to get beyond Kangding, a small city 125 miles to the west of Chengdu. This town marks the outer limit of a vast territory difficult to penetrate. For the most part, Kangding is peopled by nomads, the Khampas — an ethnic group that speaks Tibetan. Farmers and nomads, the Khampas are different in both customs and language from the Tibetans living in the center of the country. I had also been struck by their

31

coarseness, their lack of polish and amenities.

'If you need a horse,' offered one nomad who knew of my project, 'you can have mine. And me with it!'

I declined, hoping I hadn't hurt his feelings, at which point he burst out laughing. Clearly his had not been a serious offer. The fact was, I did need to buy a good horse, and it was imperative I find someone I could trust to accompany me. A student from Chengdu who worked in a tourist agency in Kangding and spoke Chinese, Tibetan, and a smattering of English responded enthusiastically to my offer. 'I'm bored with my current job,' he said. 'This is too exciting to pass up! And I don't need much money.'

We made out a list of necessary items to be purchased and mapped out our itinerary from Kangding to Derge, near the autonomous region, by the border. My plan was to travel far and wide, seeking out blind people and establishing meaningful statistics that would help me determine just how widespread blindness was in this high-altitude region, and what were its causes.

Shortly after my arrival in town, I was invited to an official government reception attended by all the local high-ranking functionaries, where I was introduced to the director of health services, the consultant for external affairs, the secretary for public affairs, and a local ophthalmologist. Tea with milk, pastries, and sweet fritters were being offered. It was pleasant enough, but despite the seeming conviviality I couldn't shake the negative feeling that had taken hold of me. In the absence of interpreters, mobilizing my fragile knowledge of Chinese and Tibetan, I struggled to articulate my project as clearly as I could.

'We are already fully aware of the project, and have asked Chengdu to start the necessary paperwork,' said one of the officials. I couldn't believe my ears. Things were moving faster than I could ever have dreamed. I hadn't even bought my horse yet.

'Does that mean I've been given the official go-ahead?'

'Not quite,' replied the consultant to foreign affairs. 'The territories you intend to visit are forbidden to foreigners. Besides, there are frequent earthquakes in these regions, not to mention landslides that wipe out the roads. And of course there's the danger of being attacked by bandits.'

'Your idea is excellent,' the ophthalmologist added emphatically. 'But in fact there isn't a single blind person in the entire region!'

'What good news!' I observed. 'Then I

guess there won't be need for my seeking funds back home to build a school for the blind!'

I had already mentioned to the authorities my efforts to collect funds for my project. I heard some of them stirring. Clearing his throat and in a very friendly voice, the governor said, 'All we're saying is, you'll have to go back to Chengdu. As soon as you receive official permission to make your trip, we'll be only too glad to endorse your project. We'll even put a four-wheel drive at your disposal, free of charge.'

The offer was more than generous, especially in the context of a region where there were no blind people! I thanked the governor and was getting ready to take my leave when the public health consultant stopped me.

'If you don't get the necessary permission back in Chengdu, perhaps you would be so kind as to transfer the funds you've already gathered to us, and we'll see what *we* can do for the blind.'

I was stunned. My project suddenly seemed to have gone down the drain. I realized nobody here believed it would really ever happen. I was completely puzzled, since I knew my project was looked upon with favor in some quarters. But since I apparently

34

had no choice, I purchased my ticket, climbed back onto the Chengdu bus, and headed back east. As it turned out, the trip was a nightmare, one of the greatest adrenaline rushes I have ever experienced: what was supposed to take sixteen hours managed to turn into thirty-three. I had fallen asleep. Apparently, as we were inching along behind a slow-moving truck, all of the sudden the forty-odd passengers began yelling at the top of their lungs. I awoke in a panic. Our driver, having had to maintain a high level of concentration along the endless narrow winding roads — some of which had been washed away — had decided to get off the bus and take a cigarette break. The only problem was, he had forgotten to put on the brake, so our bus began rolling down a sharp incline, picking up speed. The slow-moving truck that had been constantly ahead of us at the beginning of the trip, and which could have prevented us from falling farther, acting as a bumper-to-bumper buffer, had vanished into the night. We were heading straight into the abyss! Fortunately, the screaming passengers had awakened the backup driver. He jumped out of his seat and, struggling over fallen luggage, managed to grab hold of the brake and stop us from plunging over the precipice.

The passengers were now effusively thanking the backup driver for having saved their lives.

I arrived back in Chengdu completely exhausted and badly in need of a bath. Once settled back in, I began making the rounds of the local officials. The authorities here were no more encouraging than those in Kangding: 'Sorry, there's nothing we can do for you. Yes, we do like your project. Yes, we find it most interesting. What we suggest is that you contact this (or that) other department. Surely they'll be able to help you.' And so I danced from one department to the next, and back again. After several days of fruitless and frustrating efforts I went and sat on a park bench, thoroughly deflated. I needed to regroup. What in the world had happened? Had my project been too naive? Conjuring up my own words — if I remain open and flexible, good things are bound to happen — I decided I wasn't ready to give up. Not yet. At this point I heard a man ask my permission to sit down next to me. He was English, and introduced himself as Tom. 'I was in Kangding the same time you were and heard about your project,' he said. He was on a leisurely trip around the world, he told me, his next destination being Lhasa.

'Lhasa — ' I echoed. Three years before I

had gone there with my mother on our way to Kathmandu, but the high altitude had made me sick, and I spent my whole stay in bed. I remembered nothing of the city.

I told Tom about my earlier miserable visit. 'This time I'm sure you'll be fine,' he laughed. 'Your stay in Kangding, which is already eleven thousand feet high, will stand you in good stead.'

I decided to heed his sound advice. Why hang around in Chengdu when I could go directly to the Tibetan capital? Besides, he said he was off to Lhasa himself in a day or two, and I was sure he would prove helpful.

★　★　★

'Another beer?' offered Tang Lei from behind the counter of the Little Bar.

Since I was leaving very early the next morning and didn't want to miss my flight, I politely declined. My new plan was to stay in Lhasa for two months and thoroughly explore the whole region.

5

'It's always beautiful in Tibet,' I said knowingly to a young German student who was seated near me on the plane. After a year at Chengdu University, she couldn't wait for a ray of sunshine. 'The sky in Lhasa is blue, and the sun is always shining! Because Lhasa is surrounded by high mountains, there's no monsoon there.' But my meteorological expertise on Tibetan weather proved to be less than perfect: landing in Lhasa under a menacing sky, we ended up dashing from the plane to the airport terminal under a torrential rain. Forming a long line, we waited to show our documents. Even the passengers from domestic Chinese flights to Tibet — an autonomous region — are required to have their passports, visas, and various other documents examined with extreme care. This waiting time allowed me to try out the remedy Tom had suggested against high-altitude sickness. I drank one of the two bottles of mineral water bought the previous night, in which I had dissolved one tablet of effervescent aspirin. According to Tom, it was important to maintain the blood's fluidity. I had already taken a lot of liquid during the trip, not tea or coffee — both dehydrating — but sweet drinks like Coca-Cola or lemonade. Thanks to Tom's instructions, and despite being more than ten thousand feet high, I didn't feel any high-altitude malaise. My fellow German, however, had taken a recommended medication in Chengdu. Instead of thinning her blood, it had apparently had the opposite effect. First, she felt tingles at the tip of her fingers, then, on the bus, serious vertigo. Now she was suffering from terrible headaches, a typical symptom of high-altitude syndrome.

Because of a major detour it was obliged to make, the bus took about an hour and a half to get from the airport to town. The Yak Hotel had been highly recommended by all the guidebooks, but I decided to get off the bus and find a smaller inn, one more suited to my taste. I knew of several on Beijing Dong Lu, the main avenue that leads to the Potala, the Dalai Lama's winter residence.

I could already tell from the noise level that Lhasa had changed a great deal since my last visit. The wide streets and avenues that had been virtually empty three years before were now jammed with cars, all honking their horns. Little bike-taxis with their shrill bells, old wheezing trucks, and a great number of small tractors pulling containers filled to the brim with construction material and debris created a deafening cacophony.

What was more, the town was littered with garbage in high, open piles, which filled the air with the pungent odor of urine and excrement. But even more overpowering was a persistent trail of incense, mixed with various spices emanating from the surrounding restaurants.

I was appalled by the number of children in the streets tugging on my clothes, shouting, 'Gucci! Gucci!' (Money! Money!). The merchants' far too frequent 'hellos' also bothered me; I found it difficult to distinguish between a serious or helpful situation and a mere come-on to a foreigner. So when a familiar voice said 'Hello,' I didn't react immediately. The speaker decided to plant himself in front of me, barring my way. And then I realized it was Tom, who had just arrived in Lhasa a day or two before.

Thrilled to — literally — bump into someone I knew in the middle of what struck me as utter chaos, I asked Tom to help me find a place to stay. He escorted me to the Banak Shol, where he had checked in and which he liked very much. An old-fashioned inn with a traditional style, the Banak Shol was located west of Potala, near the old city, and was frequented mostly by backpacking tourists. For the equivalent of three dollars a day, I rented a room that I would share with four others. My German plane companion, who had also found her way to the Banak Shol and seemed to be getting sicker by the minute, and two English students became my roommates. The constant turnover at the Banak Shol created a lively and fun new set of friends for me.

During the next few days I explored Lhasa on my own, trying to capture its pulse. Now I was enjoying an early-morning breakfast on the roof terrace of the Banak Shol, lingering over a deliciously tart yogurt. No one was up yet, which enabled me quietly to record my diary in my dictaphone.

Next on my agenda was a walk on the Barkhor, the pilgrim path surrounding the temple of Jokhang, Lhasa's principal sanctuary as well as the spiritual center of Tibet. I had no difficulty finding the place. All I had to do was follow the labyrinth of narrow streets and let myself be carried along by the human stream that always flowed around Jokhang, being careful not to stumble over the many beggars seated or lying down along the way, or the praying monks.

Barkhor offers a rich variety of sounds, with its countless pilgrims circling the temple in a windmill of prayers. I couldn't avoid the jewelry merchants along the way, who tugged at my sleeve with their 'Looky! Looky! Cheapy, cheapy!' When I replied that, with the best intentions in the world, there was no way for me to 'looky,' they burst out laughing and moved on to their next victim.

Despite its holy reputation, Lhasa, like all cities in the world, has its fair share of merchants hawking their usual absurd tourist objects, from leather goods to an endless array of spices to plastic guns made God knows where. The merchants were lined up on either side of the sacred path, soliciting one and all, from children to young monks. I was told there was a wide variety of hats, mostly in brocade or straw, some decorated with so much fur they must have required the hide of a whole fox, feet included. Then there are the Khampas, true to their reputation, selling long sabers, leather whips, jewels, precious stones, false and real turquoise, and coral in china or plastic. A very loud stand selling alarm clocks — all ringing at the same time, as if to testify to their efficiency — was trumped by the television stores blaring along the Barkhor and the little streets around. The television sets and loudspeakers — hundreds of them, all turned up to maximum decibel — broadcast action films. The noise was such it was impossible to tell the difference between real yelling and the cries on TV boxing matches.

Part of my afternoons were spent in one of Lhasa's many monasteries. The first time I arrived at the entrance of a major monastery, I stood and listened. Despite the silence, I could feel the presence of a great many people. Quietly I sat on the stone floor, my back to the wall. Within minutes, a monk arrived with a straw mat and in a welcoming whisper reassured me that visitors like me did not disturb the monks' concentration.

Soon the crescendo of their prayers and psalms rose, interrupted by the tinkling of bells. That wonderful sonic backdrop warmed my heart. For me, it was like a radio play in which whispered texts were interspersed with ringing bells. During a meditation pause, monks passed some tea with salted butter — the traditional Tibetan beverage.

Three years before, that drink had made my mother very sick, so I cautiously put my lips to the edge of the cup. Rancid butter permeated the salty tea, and I was surprised to hear the monks swallowing it with such obvious pleasure. In Tibet one can't avoid this beverage, for it is offered constantly, on any and all occasions. I had barely started drinking, rather gingerly I confess, when a monk rushed over to refill my tin goblet to the rim. I have since got used to this mainstay Tibetan drink, and have actually come to prefer salted tea — provided it is prepared with fresh salted butter — to any other beverage, especially in cold weather.

Everything in Tibet smells of that butter. Its odor is omnipresent. Prepared from yak milk, Tibetan butter is used in all sorts of ways, starting with the cuisine but also in oil lamps, for paints and facial creams, for hair treatment, to lubricate leather and metal tools, to wax wood, and for many more things.

Most of my evenings were spent in the old city's restaurants, fraternizing with other visitors. The assortment of picturesque, and often bizarre, characters Lhasa seems to attract became a daily entertainment, from those devoted to spreading peace, to others who were simply passionate about Tibet, to people who were forever looking over their shoulders, whispering about meeting with Chinese spies and persecuted Tibetans, to the recently converted Buddhists vowing to save the world. And then there were just plain tourists, of course, some of whom found everything 'great' and 'wonderful,' while others constantly complained about everything being so hard and uncomfortable.

Frank, an Australian, belonged to the latter category. Setting out from Hong Kong, where he had found life intolerable, he arrived in Lhasa only to find the cold-water shower unbearable, the curried chicken nauseating, and, to top it off, his bed 'impossible,' because the roof leaked and his sheets and blanket were soaking wet.

One evening I met Paul, Stefan, and Biria. Biria was Israeli, and between her stint in the army and entering the university, she was exploring the world. She had arrived that morning on the same plane as Stefan, who was Czech, and Paul, who was Dutch. People who travel on their own, I have noted, are usually open to everything and seem to welcome any new contact. These three were no exception. After they had settled in at the Banak Shol, we went looking for a restaurant. Frank, the eternal complainer, joined us, and predictably, the tough yak steak he ordered gave him ample opportunity to vent his frustration. Biria chose a *bobi*, a kind of pancake filled with ground meat and vegetables, delicious but messy, offering many spilling possibilities. I would definitely never tackle a *bobi*, considering that a simple sandwich is already a challenge for me. Biria, of course, managed to spill most of the stuffing and was the butt of all sorts of jokes, which Paul was enjoying twice over, first as he witnessed it, then as he described the scene in detail for me, which made me laugh so hard I cried. As for Stefan, who was downing his rice and chicken dish with gusto, he had no inkling this would be his last meal for six weeks. The next day he contracted *giardiasis*, a kind of violent stomach illness often caught by travelers in Tibet. All the poor fellow ever saw of Tibet was the corridor from his room to the bathroom. Paul had ordered *thagap*, a traditional soup, and spent the rest of the evening entertaining us all and telling riveting tales of his past travels.

★ ★ ★

One day in the course of our extended meals on the terrace, I felt a tap on my shoulder. 'My, my! Everyone thinks you're somewhere in the wilds of Tibet taking care of the blind, when what you're really up to is stuffing your face with pancakes in this hypercivilized place!' It was Thierry, my fellow student from the University of Bonn. Despite his promise, I hadn't believed he would actually make the trip. But here he was, about to introduce the marvels of Tibet to his Chinese girlfriend. We immediately made plans to go to the warm springs near the Tidrum Nunnery, and to the old monastery of Samye, which can only be reached by boat. I also proposed going to Namtso, a fabled mountain lake. 'Why do you want to go there?' asked Frank.

'Because of the altitude. Apparently the air is exceptionally pure, and the colors of the landscape so sharp and fascinating.' As I expected, my declaration was followed by the kind of silence with which I was, alas, all too familiar. Finally mustering his courage, Paul said, 'What in the world could you find so fascinating, staring at a landscape you can't see? All landscapes must be the same for you, no? When I close my eyes, all I see is black, no matter where I am. You mean to say you see colors?'

I could have responded. But I decided to let his remark pass and hold my tongue. Of course I see colors, if only in my mind!

6

Popular opinion has it that blind people can't orient themselves, can't find their way around. Not so. What happens with us is that the other senses kick in, compensating for our unseeing eyes. To navigate in closed areas, as well as in traffic outside, the blind person relies on acoustical, olfactory, and tactile senses. In a new and unknown environment, the white cane also comes seriously into play. Swinging the cane like a pendulum, with its tip barely touching the ground, allows us to pick up all sorts of information. It enables us to determine the configuration of the ground — whether it is dry or muddy, flat or bumpy, sandy or rocky. Add to that the important acoustical information imparted by the white cane — the sound it makes when it barely touches the ground, or when we drag it, echoes differently, signaling, for example, whether we are near a building. In a narrow street, echoes allow us to understand the street's parameters, tell us if it is bordered by stone or wood buildings or by hedges or trees.

The myriad sensory signals I register make up a whole, vital information that enables me to form the blueprint of my itinerary. Let me flash forward to the time when our School for the Blind in Lhasa became a reality and describe how I get across town to reach the school. I'm aware that for most people who can see, the following details might be extremely tedious. This blueprint — created by and for me — is, however, a critical tool. Only by following scrupulously its special landmarks can I navigate seamlessly from one point to the other. These 'tedious' details are my bible.

I start at the edge of an open space. It's a square. The reason I know it's a square is from the different voices I hear — some close, some far away, and at times separated by long windows of silence. Also, the constant gurgle of a fountain, which does not give off any echoes, tells me it is not enclosed by buildings or walls.

I know the next landmark, on my right, will be a busy and noisy street. I cross the square, making sure to remain at the same distance from the sound of traffic coming from my right. The aroma of fruit — apples and pears in summer, oranges and grapefruit in winter — leads me to an alley of fruit merchants. I amble through it, carefully avoiding the customers. Continuing on, and always keeping now to the left of traffic, I walk straight until my cane bumps against the edge of the sidewalk, my next landmark. I follow that line without deviating, except when groups of people oblige me to go around them. The odor of leather, as well as the sound of constant hammering, indicates to me that I'm near a street of shoemakers. Very soon thereafter, the curbstone turns abruptly left and stops.

I know this is where the old city begins, where I can walk in the middle of the street. In the old city, cars are rare, and the few that do go through move very slowly. To my right, I always enjoy the smell of freshly baked bread, grilled meats, and noodle dishes emanating from a succession of eateries.

This street is particularly noisy, with its many television sets all going full blast. I must be one of the few people in Lhasa who actually appreciates this intolerable noise pollution, for that clamorous landmark helps me find my way. After passing the third war or martial arts film, I turn right into a small side street. I always recognize this street because of its stench — for some reason a lot of people seem to use this street as a public lavatory — and its uneven pavement, where I expect my cane to sink into deep holes, puddles, or some other even less attractive substance. At a crossroad, where the street ends in a T, I take a left. There must be a temple somewhere nearby, because in the evening a strong scent of incense permeates the air. A strong draft to my right indicates a narrow, empty passage. I remember to be particularly careful there: the street is torn up, with dangerous excavations a foot wide and several feet deep, at the bottom of which lie exposed electrical cables. When a stone wall stops me, I go left, down a small street. Only five feet wide and some forty feet long, this very narrow street apparently gives the impression, for those who can see, that the houses flanking it are so dangerously out of plumb they might tumble on top of the walker. People, I am told, are discouraged from walking through here.

Elderly men and women seated on their stoops greet me with friendly salutations, warning me of garbage piles as well as puddles. The aroma of *tchang*, the traditional Tibetan tea, and *baleb* — wafers used by Tibetans as bread; they call it *nan* bread, fresh out of the oven — hangs heavy in the street. Next I arrive at an intersection and head down a street that also ends in a T, and at that point the street to my right takes me in a zigzag to a wide avenue, with even pavement and winding turns. Traffic noise, muffled by houses until now, increases in volume.

Since many Tibetans can buy their driver's license without so much as a day's lesson, and since they don't have the slightest idea of what a red light means or that pedestrians should be given time to cross the street, I usually ask someone to help me cross. I must circle a construction site, and walk left through the next sandy path; after passing the entrance to a courtyard, left again onto a small street, then immediately right. The entrance of our school is in front of me. Some of my sighted friends actually tried following my 'blueprint' with their eyes closed and confirmed that it enabled them to find their way to the school.

★ ★ ★

Does a blind person see only darkness? is a question I am often asked. I find it illogical. If someone is completely blind, he or she can't see anything, not even darkness. A person who can see, ever so subtly, is able to perceive light and shadow and is not enveloped in darkness. Though officially blind, I never had the feeling of being in darkness. I should add, at the risk of sounding silly, that I consider myself a very visual person. I'm aware that not all blind people have visual imaginations or the ability to project images. (I'm not sure people who can see are all so gifted, either.)

Images are not the only elements imprinted in the memory. Noises and smells play an important role, and are principally what blind people register. Olfactory and auditory perceptions, as well as the sense of hot or cold, wind or calm, are translated by me into images, colored with infinite precision.

I am sure that there are sighted people who also first remember noises and smells before recalling visual forms.

Sounds help me capture people's behavior. This also holds true for gestures and other bodily movements. For instance, when a man or woman's pride has been hurt, and there is a long silence, I visualize his or her back stiff, head tilted back, nose in the air. Obviously I can't project other subtle images, such as facial expressions, veiled looks, or a nervous tic at the mouth, simply because I never experienced those when I could still see. Even when I was little, with my eyesight deteriorating, I wouldn't see such details. Colors, on the other hand, have as I mentioned always remained crystal clear to me.

Until the age of twelve, many chromatic nuances became imprinted in my memory, with the exception of what you call 'modern' colors such as electric blue, or fuchsia red. Colors become especially sharp and contrasted when I apply them to precise objects like a piece of clothing or big landscapes. When I talk about places I visited before I became blind, people are astonished that I can describe them so vividly. When I'm asked how I can possibly go into so many graphic details, I explain that it's the result of my other four senses working. To descriptions heard by others, I add in many instances my own imagination.

'So, in effect what you describe is not real!' is their answer.

What's the definition of real? Does it mean that, for sighted people, reality is limited to what their eyes see? Is priority accorded to visual impressions, which overwhelm the other sensory perceptions? Most of us possess five types of sensory perceptions. These come together and make us able to embrace the world around us. If the eye-sight is 'privileged' — as is the presumed case for those who can see — are we implying that the other senses do not contribute to the total perception of reality?

Are images captured by the eye more 'real' than those transmitted through the ear, nose, tongue, or even skin? For me, colors play such an important role in describing a landscape that I often have the feeling I am actually seeing it.

This is what happened when I visited Lake Namtso with Thierry. Namtso is a saltwater lake fifty miles long and twenty-five miles wide, 15,000 feet above sea level. According to legend, Lake Namtso is the vestige of the ancient Thetis Sea, which some 60 million years ago covered the entire Tibetan plain. And, as with Loch Ness in Scotland, over the years a rich web of legends and tales has been spun around Namtso.

In the lake's impenetrable depths, so the story goes, lives a monster that every so often lifts its nose above the surface of the blue-green waters. Intrigued by all the stories, a number of Western expeditions and teams of specialists — no place on Earth today escapes the scrutiny of science — come frequently to the lake, hoping to pierce the mystery. The extraordinary colors described by everyone who has seen the lake intrigue me more, however, than the notion that a monster dwells in its watery depths.

We drove all day over bumpy roads in a battered jeep 'made in Beijing,' when all of a sudden, after going around a rocky bend, I heard Thierry call out, 'It's here, quick, quick, a camera!' While he was busily taking shots of what he described as a 'fabulous vista,' I faced the door of the jeep, trying to picture in my own way what they were describing so enthusiastically: a beach of crystallized salt shimmering like snow under an evening sun, at the edge of a vast body of turquoise water. Farther out, the Namtso changes from turquoise to dark blue, returning to pale blue as it melts into the horizon. The setting sun was painting the surrounding mountains golden yellow, brown, and fire red. A recent downpour had frozen the mountaintops, and their peaks were covered with white powder. And down below, on the deep green mountain flanks, a few nomads were watching their yaks grazing.

My face pressed against the car window, I was enjoying it all when a slight tap from Thierry brought me back to reality.

'Do forgive me,' he said in an amused tone. 'I don't wish to sound patronizing, but if you want to see Namtso, you'd better look the other way, the lake's on the other side. What you've been staring at are rocks and a gray landscape.'

When I recount this anecdote, I'm surprised that people always react as if it's a sad story.

'Wasn't it a shock when you discovered that your fantasy had played tricks with you?'

'No,' I reply, 'it merely proves that I possess a vivid imagination, which is fine with me.'

★　★　★

Whether blessed with eyesight or blind, don't we all carry a personal notion of reality that more or less corresponds to the facts? But where and how do visual representations begin, if they haven't been recorded by the eye? In my experience, the images I have of the world are not all that different from those of people who can see. My descriptions of landscapes often appear convincing to sighted people. The principal difference, in my opinion, lies in processing the image. For example, when a normal sighted person enters a room and takes it in at a glance, he or she instantly registers the space and its contents. For a blind person, getting a sense of a new space, projecting it inside, takes a long time, for all the obvious reasons.

Whenever I enter a new space, no inner picture is immediately conjured up. I need to start exploring, touch the objects along the way. Bumping against a chair helps me feel its contours. When I touch the edge of a table with my hands, it enables me to follow its parameters and get a sense of its dimensions. All the other sensory perceptions — of the ear, nose, finger, and tongue — contribute to form a total impression that informs me of the room's general dimension, as well as its atmosphere.

For us blind, images of places or people don't necessarily coincide with what most people call reality. When I talk about a place both sighted people and I have visited, there are those who wonder whether we are actually referring to the same place. I remember one example that clearly illustrates such a discrepancy: It's fall, and I'm on horseback, riding through a forest with a friend. Close by, a blue-turquoise brook gurgles as it flows through the bushes. A light breeze gently plucks dead leaves from the path, which is covered with moss. I can't hear the horse's hoofs, because they are deadened by the moss. This is my version.

Funghow, my sighted companion, however, relates an entirely different scene: We are in front of a sawmill. Bits of crumpled paper are flying here and there as the wind lifts them off the concrete floor. What I interpret as trees in the forest are merely stacks of freshly sawed wood, which give off a pleasant smell. As for my gurgling brook, apparently a muddy canal dug in sandy soil, interrupted by wide pipes, explains the intermittent noise I register. The faint rustling of dead leaves in the breeze is, in reality, nothing more than some bits of paper scratching the cement! And to top it off, the delicious perfume of wood and resin that has me rhapsodizing about a forest simply indicates our proximity to the sawmill.

When I hear the description of that real environment, the idyllic and romantic painting my imagination has created brutally crumbles. Still, I prefer my version.

The absence of visual elements from my perception of the world creates a distinct disadvantage when I need to construct a precise and complete representation of what's happening around me. There are some compensations, however, and that absence may well prove to be an advantage, for it sharpens my four other senses.

Besides, why wouldn't a world informed and described by one's imagination be better than reality? For what it's worth, the landscapes I describe in this book are based on my very personal perception of reality. All the images I depict herein are the fruit of my imagination. Forewarned is forearmed.

7

I met Dolma, a young Tibetan woman roughly my age, on one of my morning walks along the Barkhor, a week after arriving in Lhasa.

'What are you doing out here all alone?' she asked in excellent English.

'Traveling here and there,' I replied, wishing to remain vague at this point. But quickly feeling mutual sympathy, we both decided to pursue our conversation in a small eating place nearby. Dolma ordered *momos*, a kind of fritter filled with ground yak meat and vegetables.

In the course of the meal I opened up to her and explained my hopes to open a school here for the blind.

'Your interest in the blind stems from your own condition, I assume?'

'Of course,' I replied.

'That's perfectly logical. Who can better understand the blind than a blind person herself?'

Her answer impressed me. I had had to travel halfway across the world, all the way to Tibet, to find someone — and the only one

— who thought my project was logical! Most people, no matter where, insist that the only people capable of working with the blind are pedagogues or specialists.

Dolma and I hit it off immediately. From that point on, we met regularly in the same little eatery except when I went to her home — a miserable hovel she shared with her husband, two children, and a nanny, along with what seemed to me far too many nasty rats. Unable to pronounce my name — her husband and children could only say 'Hello' to me — Dolma gave me the Tibetan name Kelsang Meto (Flower That Brings Good Luck)! My new name stuck, and to this day all my friends in Tibet know me as Kelsang Meto.

A medical adviser, Dolma travels to faraway farms and villages, teaching farmers and nomads basic notions of hygiene and preventive medicine. Confirming a fact I had long suspected, she told me that blindness is prevalent in the autonomous region of Tibet basically because of its unusually high altitude. The principal cause of blindness there is children's exposure to ultraviolet rays. Nomads and farmers living on that high plateau have no way to protect themselves against the strong rays of the sun.

'With so many blind children, there must

be a number of institutions providing help for them, no?' I ventured.

'No,' Dolma quickly replied. 'None. But I have a feeling things will change with your arrival.'

'Not so fast!' I told her. I still had a lot to learn about everything in Tibet, the people, the country, their living conditions, and so much more. 'How do blind people actually get along in Tibet?' I asked.

When I asked my professor back in Germany the same question, he had replied with a deep sigh that blind people in Tibet lived with their eyes shut. 'They sleep all day long!' is how he put it.

'I can't really believe that,' I said, horrified. 'Do *I* sleep all day long?'

'You're a special case, Sabriye!'

Dolma proceeded to fill me in on a number of important details. Her grim report depressed me. In the nomad camps she had visited, she had observed different patterns, different situations. In some communities, blind children were given small tasks, depending on their capabilities, and as a result were reasonably well integrated into local society. In most other camps, however, the blind were totally abandoned, relegated to the far end of their huts, living in the dark, surviving hand-to-mouth from relatives and neighbors. Marginal citizens.

A number of more entrepreneurial nomads came to realize that blindness could actually be turned into a lucrative business, and many of them moved to the city. Entire families migrated to Lhasa, obliging their blind children to go into the streets and beg. Those children, once living like vegetables, often became the sole means of support for entire Tibetan families, precious commodities for a large segment of the blind population.

According to popular belief in Tibet, blindness is a punishment meted out for bad deeds committed in a previous life. Worse yet, many today throughout the country are still convinced that the blind are possessed by the devil, that they are cursed and dangerous. Armed with extrasensory perception, the blind are presumed to perceive things hidden from the seeing world. This explains why today blind people are so often avoided in Tibet. In some parts of the country, there are those who are convinced that merely touching a blind person will render them impure.

The lamas, for their part, deep in their study of Buddhism, view blindness from a whole other perspective. For them, any handicap — and blindness is no exception

— constitutes a precious advantage. Addressing adversity fortifies a person's spirit.

Shortly after our talk, Dolma suggested I conduct my own investigation. Leading me to a crowded, bustling place at noon, she brought over a little blind girl who told us she had lost her sight when her family's house had burned down. They had subsequently moved to the city, and her aunt was sending her each day out into the street to earn their daily bread. That seemed perfectly normal to her.

As if she had overheard us, the aunt appeared out of nowhere, admonishing Dolma for interfering, ordering her to let the girl go. 'She's worried about her income!' remarked Dolma bitterly. Grabbing the girl quickly, the aunt marched her charge off to where work could proceed undisturbed.

A little bike-taxi took Dolma and me to Potala. In the park, right behind the Dalai Lama's palace, surrounded by an applauding audience, a young guitar player was performing. 'This is Tashi,' Dolma explained. 'He's blind and composes beautiful songs. Everyone in Lhasa, in fact in the whole region, knows him.' I walked over to his coin cup and, leaning over, added a few coins of my own.

'Can he really survive by his music?' I asked.

'And how!' she said. 'Tashi does very well. He's respected and accepted precisely because he earns his living. Unlike most other blind people, he has not become a charge to his family or the community.'

We stood there enjoying his playing for a while before returning to the center of town. Navigating carefully, with the help of Dolma, through narrow, winding, and highly odoriferous streets, backyards, and alleys, with dirty hanging sheets and plastic bags strewn everywhere, we stopped at the foot of a rickety set of stairs. Climbing to the top floor, we found ourselves in a room with only two walls. In place of the two missing walls, blankets were hung as sole protection against wind, snow, or rain. Seated on a cushion on the dirt floor, an old woman greeted us. With a great sense of hospitality, she stood as soon as we entered, offering us her cushion.

She had had five sons — all blind, she told us immediately. Her husband had long ago abandoned them. Apparently, many men in Tibet react in the same way when a child is born or becomes blind. A blind offspring often represents dishonor, a curse to the father.

Dolma explained I had traveled all the way

from Europe to assess the situation of the blind in Tibet. Excited, the old woman called out to her youngest son, who arrived running.

'This is Migmar, the only family member who earns any money,' Dolma informed me. His mother asked him to take us to his brothers. And without the help of a cane, he moved right along — practically sprinting, making it hard for us to keep up — through other narrow, winding streets.

Walking ahead of us, he clapped his hands or snapped his fingers. I knew this was his way of testing the space around him, a trick I recognized and had often practiced myself. Depending on the echo, you are able to determine whether you're in a courtyard or a square. The snapping or clapping sound can signal the presence of objects along or paintings on the walls, depending on the depth of the echo.

We followed Migmar into a low-ceilinged tavern. A strong smell of *tchang*, the local beer that tastes like lemon soda and goes down deceptively easily, was overpowering. We weaved in and out of a drunken group of men seated at low tables, loudly pursuing a game of mah-jongg, while a number of women, in charge of checking the men's glasses, were fussing, making sure the glasses were constantly filled.

Migmar pointed out his four brothers, all of whom were squatting, glass in hand. He tried introducing us to them, but they seemed completely uninterested and showed no reaction whatsoever. Undeterred, we took a seat next to them, and Dolma ordered a cool *tchang*. She offered a beer to Migmar, but he declined.

He had stopped drinking alcohol, he told us, after observing the toll it had taken on his brothers, who had become entirely dependent on the goodwill of neighbors, and lived like vegetables. The silence of these young men eloquently betrayed their despair and resignation; Migmar, on the contrary, seemed perfectly cheerful and content.

'Many neighbors give me their old radios to repair,' he told us proudly. 'And from that I manage to earn my living.' And then, very timidly, he added, 'If only I knew how to speak Chinese or English, I could earn a lot more money!'

'Did you ever consider going to school?' asked Dolma.

'Of course. A long time ago I attended the same school as my cousins. But the teacher asked me to leave because I wasn't learning as fast as the rest of the class.'

This was the moment I had been waiting for.

'There is a special language for the blind, you know.'

Since the start of the trip, I had been carrying with me a large pouch under my jacket, containing a few pages of the Tibetan braille alphabet I had devised. On the thick sheets were stamped the thirty basic characters of the alphabet for the blind. My teacher in Bonn had helped me trace the corresponding characters in Tibetan.

Dolma started reading aloud to Migmar the sounds of that syllabic alphabet while I guided his fingers over the little points in relief.

'How strange!' he said. 'How strange that you come from so far away to teach us writing in our very own tongue!'

I wasn't organized yet — my school hadn't been set up to take Migmar in. And it saddened me to bid him good-bye. I knew however, that he would do fine. As for his brothers, it was too late; they were too old, too far gone.

8

One afternoon, back in Germany where I was studying Central Asian civilization, a fellow student entered the library and started shouting, 'What in hell is this noise all about? No one can work or concentrate with this damn machine! What is this anyway, a dentist's office?'

Bang! The library door slammed shut behind him. I felt directly targeted. Five students had already departed in a huff that afternoon, leaving me alone with my 'reading machine.' I admit, this machine is offensively loud, and definitely intrusive for a library. What could I do, though?

The machine I'm referring to is called an Optacon and is made in America. It has a little camera attached to it. The camera reads the printed characters, and a contraption with small needles translates them into pulses, which are sent to my left index finger. This is how I and other blind people are able to read.

This reading process is not only very difficult, it has the serious disadvantage of being extremely loud. The student was absolutely right: the machine makes a noise reminiscent to that of the dentist's loud drills.

'Think long and hard before you sign up for these courses,' my professor had warned me as he watched me immersed in my studies at the library. 'You're the first blind person to tackle the Tibetan language. Many sighted students give up after the first semester. Besides, do you know in your heart of hearts *why* you want to study Tibetan?'

All my professors were the same: nice enough but not at all encouraging. On the very first day of class the director gave us the following opening speech: 'It always pleases me to see each year the growing interest in Central Asian studies, and Tibet in particular. Nonetheless, I must bring your attention to the fact that the study of Tibet opens no possibilities for future jobs, and in addition, it is extremely difficult.'

Apart from stubborn students, or picturesque amateur Buddhists convinced their study, and some time spent in a monastery in Tibet or India, would guarantee them nirvana, this opening speech did manage to discourage a fair number of students, who from that day on simply didn't bother showing up for class. Even among those fanatic Buddhists — for me recognizable by their incense or aromatic oils — quite a few suddenly vanished into thin air as well, no doubt opting for meditation.

Why *was* I complicating my life? I often asked myself during that first semester. Wouldn't philosophy and sociology have suited me just as well? Given my situation, it would have been so much easier, certainly sparing me from having to painstakingly decipher characters from an unknown alphabet. In other disciplines, all that would have been required was for someone to read me the class program, which I would then have translated into braille with the help of a computer.

But in the department of Central Asian studies, no one was equipped for or capable of reading my course list. No software for Tibetan studies existed. I was therefore obliged to spend untold hours decoding unknown characters with the help of the Optacon, until my left index became numb and my ears buzzed from the dreadful noise made by the machine.

Ultimately, not wishing to disturb my professors and fellow students during class, I stopped using my reading machine and tried memorizing versions and themes as best I could. This worked fine at first, but as texts got more complicated and difficult to retain, I gave up and ended up sitting passively in class.

Couldn't they tape their required texts? I pleaded with my professors.

Unfortunately, pronunciation in Tibetan is such that a phoneme can lead to several characters. If many words have almost identical pronunciation, they also have different spellings.

I often found myself despairing, but nevertheless vowed, stubborn person that I am, not to give up. Tibetan studies had been my obsession since eighth grade in high school in Marburg. Back then, my schoolmates — all blind or with declining eyesight — and I were taken one day to an exhibit on Tibet. To help us fully appreciate the exhibit, the curator opened the glass cases and invited us to touch various objects such as weapons, prayer beads, and wooden sculptures. I let my fingers explore these art objects, wonderfully exotic to me, some made of metal, others of wood or carved bone. We learned a great deal about Tibet's customs, history, and religion that day. I was immediately fired up. Eager to learn more, I asked where I could pursue studies in Tibetan language and culture. The University of Bonn had a Department of Central Asian studies, the curator told me. My conversation with that man that day turned out to be critical for me. I had found my vocation.

When I told my teachers about my new ambition, they were cool to the idea. 'Why not study history where there is ample braille material for you?' was the most encouragement I got.

'Absurd!' exclaimed another professor to whom I outlined my elaborate plans for going to Tibet, and my dream of founding a school for the blind there. 'Don't give that project another thought,' he said. Then, tempering his tone, he added, 'At least don't try to do it on your own. Why not contact the Red Cross?'

So I did. It turned out the Red Cross never allows handicapped or blind people to work in the field, or for any of their foreign missions. That struck me as odd, since who better than a handicapped person can understand the needs and wants of another? That day was the first of many where I simply refused to take no for an answer. I decided to find some way — there had to be one, I was sure — to help the blind in Tibet. On my own. And today, several years later, thanks to my persistence — or my obsession, you might say — I have developed techniques and methods that facilitate those very studies in Tibetan.

I realized that my 'reading machine' no longer sufficed. I needed to find a way to adapt braille to the Tibetan alphabet. As yet, there was no braille in that language. I decided to give it a try — immediately. As a starting point, I followed the traditional braille, in which the Latin alphabet and numbers are represented by one or several points in relief — each forming a grid of three points, in two vertical rows that can be compared to the digit 6 on a die.

These six points can form sixty-four combinations, a sufficient number to transcribe most of the world's alphabets.

A	B	C	D	E	F	G	H	I	J
K	L	M	N	O	P	Q	R	S	T
U	V	W	X	Y	Z				

To apply braille to Tibetan, I needed to pay attention to the peculiarities of syllabic writing in Tibetan. The Tibetan alphabet has thirty consonants. When a syllabic consonant is not accompanied by a vowel mark, it is followed by the sound *ah*. Most syllabic characters as well as their corresponding monosyllabic phonemes correspond to a word, each with its own meaning. For example, *kha* means 'mouth,' *ra* means 'goat.'

Mouth   Goat

The consonants of the Tibetan alphabet can also appear in odd structural groups. There is always a principal consonant, around which other consonants gravitate, and onto which the vowels *i, u, e,* and *o* are added through the use of special marks; these can also be placed over or under the principal consonant.

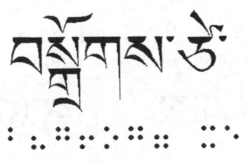

Table

Because these configurations would take too much space in the conventional braille system, I had to resort to the traditional Latin transcription, which places one or more consonants superimposed before the principal one, and the minor consonant below — the complementary vowels being in turn placed after the minor consonant.

The development of this system helped considerably. In the beginning, I read new texts with the Optacon machine. I could then transpose them without difficulty in a form that was directly accessible to me. As I read, I would dictate syllable by syllable into my recording machine, and transpose the cassette into braille. It isn't as complicated as it might seem. The spelling of the Tibetan language is fairly complex, but for centuries Tibetans have devised a system of rhythmic spelling that allows any text to be swiftly dictated.

With the help of a braille writing machine, adapted to Tibetan, I could write seamlessly under dictation, and often even faster than the sighted students. After writing down new words on separate little cards, I would classify them in alphabetic order. This way, I created my own Tibetan-German/German-Tibetan dictionary in braille. It pleased me no end to help some of my sighted classmates verify words.

Later I worked with a blind mathematician who helped me develop software capable of transposing Tibetan texts from Latin tran-scription into braille, with the help of a special printer. Thanks to that software, today — several years later — an increasing number of books have become accessible and available to blind Tibetans.

But we weren't there yet. As a first-year student, I was far from imagining that my little invention would one day help so many blind people beyond myself. As it turned out, it took many semesters for professors and heads of Central Asian departments to take an interest in it, accept it, and implement it in their courses.

A scholar of Tibetan studies at the University of Bonn asked me one day to present my system to him. He often visited the autonomous region of Tibet, he said, and his mission was to help found and financially support schools in eastern central Tibet. He was interested in presenting my Tibetan braille to the local cultural authorities, adding, 'It might even be possible for you one day to go present this process in Tibet.'

It had long been a dream of mine to go to Tibet and make a mark for myself. I couldn't imagine anything more worthwhile than introducing and teaching my reading/writing method to the blind of Tibet!

I was well aware that foreigners are not allowed to work in the autonomous region of Tibet, but I couldn't help but be bitterly disappointed when the distinguished professor, upon his return from Tibet, told me, 'They were immensely interested in your method, but when I suggested they invite you to demonstrate your invention, they were reticent.'

'What did they really say?' I asked.

'They don't believe a blind person would be sufficiently independent to succeed in such an endeavor.'

Once again, I refused to let myself be discouraged. Dammit! I *would* find a way!

9

Hardworking and fazed by nothing, the unflappable Dolma continued to prove a precious ally. When I told her of my intention of traveling through the countryside on horseback to present my method to the blind, her reaction was immediately enthusiastic. We decided to start with the Drigung district. According to what pilgrims from that region had told us, there were many blind children there, and ophthalmologists had confirmed it. One of the reasons was the diet in Drigung: it was particularly lacking in vitamin A, which exacerbated potential blindness in young children.

Drigung is about a hundred miles from Lhasa. It would take us approximately ten days on horseback, Dolma figured.

'You know how to ride a horse?' I asked her as we were taking our walk on the Potala. We had planned to rent two or three horses from those on display for tourists.

'Of course!' she answered quickly.

I was immediately ashamed and felt myself blushing. How could I have asked her such a question? By definition, all Tibetans are excellent riders. In fact, they often ride before they learn how to walk.

Buying or renting a horse in Tibet is no small matter, especially for a foreigner. Not only do prices immediately skyrocket, but as a foreigner one has to be careful not to be left with an old nag.

'Ten days!' exclaimed one of the owners. His shouting had drawn a little crowd. 'After ten days, my horses will return worn out with their hoofs broken, and I won't be able to sell them to anyone!' He was asking for a small fortune per day, per horse. Quickly doing the math in my head, I came to the conclusion that for the same amount he was charging me, we could buy ten good horses.

In the crowd that had gathered was a *pola* (in Tibet, most old men are called *pola*, 'grandfather'). Taking Dolma aside, he asked her why we needed these horses. A trip in a jeep would be so much easier, he assured us, and so much more comfortable. Dolma didn't answer, but I shook my head. I do not enjoy traveling at high speed, and in a jeep, the window separates one from the outside world; in my particular case, it would deprive me of the necessary sounds and smells that inform me about an environment. Furthermore, in a jeep you're obliged to follow roads or dry riverbeds. Even an all-terrain jeep can't really make it up some hills or soft inclines, or reach remote hard-to-get-to villages, whereas a horse can cross difficult roads and mountains, go virtually anywhere. *Pola* understood. 'You can have two of my horses, plus an extra packhorse,' he said. 'My mother is blind. She would have loved to learn how to read and write. All I ask is that you feed my animals well, and return them to me in good shape.'

I was overwhelmed by his generosity. For some reason, Dolma didn't seem to share my enthusiasm. I couldn't understand why she remained so passively silent.

We needed to make some preparations. We rushed to the Barkhor to gather the provisions we needed for the trip. Dolma bought a sack of wheat flour and some dried yak meat. Would that be enough for ten days? I wondered.

Back at Banak Shol, I recounted our little adventure to Biria. 'What a fantastic story!' she said. 'You wouldn't by any chance have an extra horse for me, would you? If you don't, it's all right, I could follow you on a bike!'

I didn't know what to make of her proposition. Wasn't one foreigner — 'Long Nose,' as Tibetans called foreigners — and a 'Long Nose' led by a blind one to boot, enough on this expedition? This said, there was no question that we could definitely use an extra hand feeding the horses. It was agreed: Biria would join us, by any mode of transportation, whether by horse or by bike.

The next morning found the three of us in a state of great excitement. Each of us was carrying a knapsack of provisions and a sleeping bag strapped to the back of the saddle. As for the tent I had purchased at Dolma's suggestion, especially for the expedition, we decided to leave it behind. Farmers along the way would surely offer us a place to sleep, she assured us.

At the appointed time, Pola arrived at the inn with his two horses and the packhorse. To our delight, he had even decorated each horse with multicolored ribbons and a string of little bells. The traditional wooden saddles, covered with a thick rug, were fastened by superb braided leather straps. A colt accompanied the white mare. 'Why did you bring this colt?' we asked.

'I am worried the colt will feel abandoned without its mother,' was Pola's response.

First we hoisted our luggage onto the packhorse. When everything was solidly fastened, I climbed onto the white mare, and Pola handed me the lead shank of the packhorse. Meanwhile, I noticed — and still didn't understand why — Dolma was circling the horse instead of mounting it. She was so small and slight, perhaps that was the problem? Pola offered to hoist her up, but Dolma, with tears in her voice, walked away and blurted, 'I have to confess — I don't know how to ride a horse!'

This was shocking to me. Jumping off my mare, I decided we needed to regroup quickly. 'Let's take our luggage off the horses,' I said, 'and we'll decide what to do.'

Devastated and ashamed, Dolma was sitting pathetically on a low wall as a small crowd gathered around us. Fully aware that not being able to ride in Tibet was tantamount to being dishonored, I was consoling her as best I could. Biria was making some effort to help Dolma regain her composure, and I to lighten the atmosphere, when Pola interrupted us.

'If it would help the cause, I'd be happy to come along!' he offered. That struck us as the perfect solution. He accepted our small monetary offer, and we agreed to leave the following day. Dolma, too, had agreed to overcome her shame and ride on a slow horse, learning as she went.

As we departed the next morning, we must have formed an impressive caravan. Pola, on his black, rambunctious stallion, which looked ready to bite anyone crossing him, was wearing the traditional and colorful Khampa costume. In addition to the three horses and the colt, Pola had brought a special horse along for Biria.

Word had spread all around town, and the Banak Shol interior courtyard as well as the neighboring sidewalks were packed with people who had come to wish our little caravan 'Bon voyage,' 'Ahzi,' and 'Ozi-ah!'

We left the city behind, and as soon as we found ourselves in fields and wider spaces, we all started relaxing. The only sounds we could hear were those of crows flying over our heads, the muffled impact of horseshoes tramping on the soft ground, and the constant high-pitched tinkling of the many little bells on our horses, which increased in volume as our horses gained speed.

Dolma's horse was trotting slowly, and we were all pleased and proud to see that with each passing mile she was growing more and more confident and accustomed to riding, holding herself proud and high. Though it took her longer than the rest of us, she too was beginning to relax.

Our first stop was near a small river. We removed the luggage and the saddles and led our horses down to drink. It didn't take long before a group of farmers had gathered around us. Curious, they asked us all sorts of questions.

'Who are you?'

'Are you really here to help our blind?'

'And how are you planning to do that?'

Satisfied by our answers, they offered to take care of our horses, which they did with great expertise. As we were sitting on the grass chewing on dry yak meat, the farmers' wives arrived carrying large tin pots of tea with smoking-hot butter. Despite my distaste for hot buttered tea, I accepted a cup. To refuse would have been insulting.

* * *

Whenever I am asked to describe Tibetan cuisine, I always say that for Europeans accustomed to delicious, varied, and sophisticated food, traditional Tibetan cuisine might not do. The combination of local needs, limited and meager resources, and the high altitude that dictates the local diet does not offer much room for creative cuisine. To keep food longer than a season, Tibetans finely slice and dry yak and lamb meat. The hot, salty buttered tea — which takes some getting used to — has the virtue of warming one in winter and preventing dehydration in summer. The little bit of fat from the yak butter is also a source of precious energy. *Tsampa* — a dough made from roasted barley, buttered tea, and a bit of cheese, rolled into small balls and eaten raw — constitutes another type of food with important nutrients, particularly appreciated by Tibetans. A kind of daily fare, and by no means a delicacy, the *tsampa* always proves handy when traveling in the wilds for several days, or roaming the desert.

During our little picnic, more women and children had gathered around us. As we were explaining in greater detail the purpose of our journey, a *mola* (an affectionate name for a grandmother) leaned over to Dolma, and with broad gestures and in a language I couldn't understand told her of a family nearby with sixteen-year-old twins — both blind. Their parents were terribly upset, she explained, because of the twins' inability to learn any kind of profession.

'The village is not far off the road to Drigung,' she told us. 'You could make it there without too much of a detour.'

We first went over a high mountain pass and followed the Kichu River. A burning sun prevented us from advancing rapidly, and as for the path — when there was one — it was in terrible shape. To reach the village, we had to go up and down steep hills or, reining in our horses, dismount and wade through waist-high water. Meanwhile, the two-month-old foal of my mare kept coming to a halt every other step. Sniffing at the haystacks along the sides of the path, he would start whining miserably. Its mother, after stopping as well, would prick up her ears and, neighing loudly, trot over to her foal.

We had to stop three times on that journey to let our horses drink from the river, eat beans and grass. The village we were trying to reach was still miles away, and Pola was concerned there would not be enough to feed the horses — grass grew only near villages. Meanwhile, evening was approaching, and we needed to find a place for the night. But villagers, we were told, weren't allowed to take us in. A strict Tibetan law forbade natives from inviting foreigners into their homes. Why hadn't we known this? I was sorry to have left my tent behind in Lhasa.

We had reconciled ourselves to seeking refuge under the ledge of a rock when a friendly villager who had heard of our needs invited us to take shelter in his hut. He took no chances, quickly sending one of his sons to ask the head of his village for permission to welcome us for the night. After being offered salted tea and cool *tchang*, we settled on wooden benches covered with rugs, and straw mats that served both as seats and beds. In Tibet, rugs are a family's most precious possession. These, however, were badly frayed, with big holes in them. Our host, clearly delighted to be with people he could talk to, wasted no time telling us his wife had recently died, and he was raising his three children alone. The youngest one had just turned two, and the twelve-year-old, who had finished school, was helping him in the fields.

The head of the village arrived and, after bowing dramatically several times, thanked us profusely for what we were doing for Tibet. I smiled. What had we done so far? Not much, really, I thought. Till now, all we had to show was a long hot summer ride on horseback. But I knew it was too early to judge.

The two men started talking, and after much whispering, the head of the village bowed and left the hut.

'You have just been given the green light to stay with me for the night,' our host announced cheerfully. In reality, we would have much preferred to park our luggage and ourselves outside in the courtyard, where there was some kind of awning, but he insisted we spend the night in the hut. He and his sons would sleep outside.

None of us slept a wink that night. Inside the hut, the stench of rat and vermin droppings was unbearable. As soon as we turned off our lamp, we could hear those dreadful rodents getting noisily to work. We could hear scratching sounds coming from the oven, followed by the little pitter-patter of rat feet. They were having a field day. I wasn't.

Buddhism forbids killing any living creature. As a result, no one in Tibet feels in the least inconvenienced by parasites. I resigned myself and zipped myself up tight inside my sleeping bag, feeling quite protected from the persecuting intruders. I was wrong. Before long I began itching all over, and after spending half the night trying to locate the origin of the bites, exhausted, I finally fell into a deep sleep. In the morning, shaking out my sleeping bag, I discovered a number of dead fleas. As for myself, I was covered with bites.

We were treated to tea with rancid butter for breakfast. In contrast to us in our pitiful state, our hosts seemed in fine fettle. This had been the first night they had all slept so well, away from the rats and insatiable fleas.

We quickly rose and thanked our host, prepared our horses, and were ready to leave when the head of the village we had seen the previous night reappeared. Would we please follow him? He took us to another hut at the

90

edge of the village, where we found an old woman sitting on the edge of a bed. She was holding a small child on her lap — her little four-year-old blind granddaughter. The child had never been taught to walk.

When we learned the child's age, we gasped. She seemed like an overgrown infant. 'Why has she never walked?' we asked. As far as we could determine, there was nothing wrong with her legs.

Dolma and I stood there, appalled. Hiding her face in shame, the grandmother told us that to keep the little girl from hurting herself when they went out into the fields or to tend the livestock, they had to tie her to the mattress.

Pulling back the child's blanket, Dolma discovered to her horror a little girl who was nothing but skin and bones. Her body had never developed. Not only had she never been taught to walk but her poor little legs were no more than matchsticks.

'This is unacceptable!' Dolma stormed. 'You must start massaging the little girl's legs every day, starting right now. Every day! I'll show you exactly how to do it! Only if you massage her regularly is there any hope your grandchild will ever walk.' She sat down beside the child and proceeded to demonstrate how to massage her legs. 'I'll come back to check on your progress in a few weeks,' she warned.

'But she's blind! How can she ever walk?' the old woman asked.

Dolma's patience was growing thin; I could hear the change in her voice. Angrily, she pointed at me and said, 'Kelsang Meto over there is blind! But she walks, travels, runs, even rides *horses!*'

That seemed to impress the old woman. She promised to follow Dolma's instructions about massaging and help her granddaughter learn to walk.

We left terribly upset by what we had witnessed, wondering how many more such cases lay hidden throughout the country. Back on our horses, we left for the mountains, prospecting for blind children in further villages.

Still tired from the previous day's travels, our horses seemed lethargic. Pola's method of spurring them on was to make cracking sounds with his whip. But that failed to produce any positive results. Instead of galloping faster, the horses simply stopped and bucked, as if ready to bite their tormentor. Pola ran around taunting them, seemingly enjoying his teasing. He was torturing the poor animals, we felt, and we refused to share his apparent amusement.

Meanwhile the horses were getting wilder and wilder. We shouted to Pola to stop. With each crack of his whip, my typically Western notion that all Tibetans treat animals with care and respect was smashed to smithereens. If only the horses would bite Pola's rear end, I thought, it would teach him a good lesson! Just then one of the horses caught Dolma's foot and wouldn't let go of it. Dolma was screaming at the top of her lungs, finally bringing Pola to his senses. Dropping his whip, he walked over to his stallion, who was watching from a safe distance, snorting nervously.

But when Pola tried to swing himself onto the saddle, I heard a loud neigh, immediately followed by a thump. The galloping sounds that followed told me the horse had run away, leaving Pola on the ground. I could hear Biria and Dolma break into malicious and uncontrollable laughter. The horse had raced around in circles, as they described it to me, rid himself of the old man, and run off. Quickly recovering from his fall, Pola tried catching the wild horse. After some time and effort, he finally did. But as soon as Pola tried to hoist himself back up onto the saddle, the horse started bucking furiously again. We all dismounted. Holding our horses' reins, each of us attempted to calm

93

our scared and sweaty charges.

As we finally approached the village the *mola* had mentioned to us the first day, we were greeted by a large group of children who ran up to us, laughing and shouting.

'Our village chief has been expecting you,' one little girl told us, dancing cheerfully.

How had he learned about our visit? This was always a source of wonder for us. How could they, from miles away, have heard of us? There were obviously no telephones in any of these remote villages, and only occasionally did vehicles — aware of the risk those rocky, worn-down roads represented — venture into them. How in the world did news travel from village to village? We were puzzled. We never elucidated that mystery.

After welcoming us, the chief led us to a big house where a family with their two blind children lived. In contrast to the previous night's spare cabin, this large house had many rooms with a narrow corridor. We followed her through the labyrinth. No rancid butter and mildew odor here. An inviting aroma of incense and sweet fritters permeated the house.

We found the two blind brothers sitting side by side on top of a low wall. Looking frightened, they did not even respond to Dolma's efforts to engage in conversation.

'Would you be interested in learning the new writing for blind people?' their mother asked them.

'No,' was their chorused response.

Turning back to us, she continued, 'Ever since they were little boys, their main occupation has been sitting next to each other on that same wall. I worry that they're too old now to learn anything — and probably too scared to leave the house.'

Another sad, frustrating visit. The mother was right — by the time our school would officially start, the boys would be too old for our program.

We continued on to Drigung. Wherever we passed, villagers were already expecting us, often assembled at the highest point of the village to view the unusual spectacle we must have made entering their village: there we were, one richly dressed Tibetan on a black stallion leading the way, followed by three women all dressed differently, riding horses decorated with bells and multicolored ribbons! Once again, we were mystified how news traveled so fast — faster than we did, it seemed.

At Drigung, a group of people led us to a blind child's home. On the way there, a young man ran up to me, begging me to come and cure his blind grandmother.

'I'm not a doctor, and I'm blind myself,' I told him.

'Please!' he begged again.

'I'm terribly sorry, but as much as I'd like to, there's no way I can cure your grandmother,' I said.

He walked away, clearly upset and disappointed.

* * *

Six miles from Drigung, Dolma's horse began to limp. Exhausted by the heat and the rough and rocky paths, the mare eventually simply refused to go on. Pola was the only one able to get her to budge. Not without a certain malicious afterthought, he suggested Dolma ride his stallion. But Dolma was quick to refuse; like her mare, she stood, refusing to take one step farther.

I had taken a liking to Nagpo, the black 'devil,' from the very first. So I asked the old man if I could try my luck with his horse.

'Absolutely not!' Pola cried, terrified. 'Nagpo is dangerous, he could buck you off.'

'So what?' I asked.

'You can't,' Biria joined in, 'you're blind. It would be unwise.'

That kind of illogical response makes me furious. I had been riding horses since I was a child, and very often had to deal with difficult ones. I also knew it would have been absurd to force a terrified beginner to mount this kind of horse. But I was no terrified beginner. Finally, Pola gave in and put his whip in my hand. And I handed it right back to him. Passing me the reins, he stepped back carefully. I was a little nervous, I admit, feeling pressure to succeed. Slowly, feeling my way, guided by the reins, I approached the stallion from one side and cautiously held my hand flat out in front of his muzzle. He remained still, then carefully and slowly started sniffing my hand. With as calming a voice as I could, I muttered some nonsense into his ear. Biria couldn't suppress a giggle, which frightened the horse, who lifted his head. Not letting that disturb me, I carried on with my whispering. After a few minutes, Nagpo slowly calmed down. I felt him relax, and carefully climbed up onto the saddle. After a brief pause — I didn't want to press my luck — I squeezed my thighs gently. Nagpo moved forward, hesitantly at first, and soon picked up speed, the other horse in tow. After their little break, they followed their leader without any problem.

In Dolma's and Biria's eyes, this seemed a small miracle. They had already resigned themselves, pictured me lying in the grass trampled by hooves. As for Pola, he did not appreciate my taming his wild horse. Male pride? Over the next few days, he went out of his way to make my life, as well as that of the horse, miserable. He would sneak up from behind and crack his whip, so that Nagpo would rise up, first on his hind legs then on his front, then career around the next corner with me clinging to the saddle. Strange old man, that Pola.

Near the Drigung district border, we decided to leave the horses in Pola's care for one night. They badly needed the rest. Besides, there was a good road to Drigung, if we were lucky, we'd be able to hitch a ride from a truck and quickly reach our destination.

As we arrived in this small village, we were greeted by the head man, who had heard of our imminent arrival through the invisible news network. He was standing in the street, waving *katags* — white scarves for good luck — which he promptly placed around our necks as a form of welcome. He had already sent the postman to two blind children families, to inform them of our arrival.

Our first stop was a house where a man lived with his five-year-old blind son.

The boy, whose name was Kunchog, seemed very alert and curious. I quickly explained to him what braille was, and he wasted no time asking if he could inspect the braille material I had brought along. I guided his finger over the dots; when I explained that the dots represented letters, he squealed with joy. His father, as curious and intrigued as his son, sat down beside us, watching my demonstration with awe. Since he could read and write himself, he was able to understand the system very quickly. They both expressed the desire to learn braille.

'Where could Kunchog learn this?' the father asked.

'Kelsang Meto is preparing to open a school in Lhasa for all the blind children of Tibet,' Dolma explained. 'There, any blind child can come and learn braille.'

I was a little frightened. Wasn't she promising too much or too soon? I hadn't even come to an agreement with the authorities to teach in Tibet, and judging from my little experience in China and Tibet, anything could happen. I had to remind Dolma that there was preliminary research. More concrete plans would follow later.

'You can do it,' Dolma said. 'You've already made it this far.' Then, turning to the father: 'We'll let you know as soon as our school opens.'

We went on to another family. In the

courtyard of a farmhouse, an eight-year-old boy, his little sister, his parents, and his grandmother were all sitting in a row on a wooden bench. When the boy, Chila, heard us coming, he jumped up, ran toward us, and led us to the middle of the courtyard, where he started feeling our clothes and bombarding us with all sorts of questions. 'Are you coming here to help me see? To help me be like other children?'

All this time, both his parents and grandmother remained seated, stock still. In an attempt to break the ice, I took out the braille alphabet quietly and began explaining it to them. No success. They still showed not the slightest interest. Silent as statues.

'Kelsang Meto has come from very far away to build a school for blind children in Lhasa,' said the head of the village, coming to my rescue.

'A school!' echoed Chila, who started jumping up and down, again. 'Pala, Amala, I want to go to school!'

Only then did the parents begin to thaw. The father stood up and, fetching a bowl of butter tea with a little bread, turned to me: 'The teacher in our village did not allow us to send our boy to school,' he said hesitantly. 'We had given up all notion of an education for our son. Your visit and the prospect of your school is like a dream for us. It's hard and wonderful to believe our son will actually be entering school.' Chila came over to me, and we sat down together. As I began explaining to him certain braille symbols, his mother said, 'Because you're also blind, we know you sincerely care about the blind. We'd very much like you to come back when you're ready, and take Chila as a full-time boarder to your school in Lhasa.'

We were delighted. We were actually beginning to line up future students! Now all that was required was a school! We had a long way to go, I knew, but each day brought us nearer. Still, I also knew we were only advancing inch by inch.

10

To this day, Dolma is convinced that we only avoided the *dres* by a hair's breadth. She doesn't like talking about that night, apparently out of embarrassment; after all, she's a modern, educated woman. But I know that's not the real reason she doesn't want to talk about it. Dolma is afraid the demons will notice us again if we talk about them, and they are angrier today than they were then.

'Then' was the night we were lodged in the 'guest house' of the village chief, a stable of sorts with two small slits for windows and a wooden door that hung loosely on its hinges and rattled frightfully with every gust of wind. The hut was at the edge of the village, tucked under an overhanging ledge. Toward evening an old monk had escorted us there, leaving us a small butter lamp.

Biria and I became aware of Dolma's hesitation even before we stepped into the guest house. 'What's the matter?' we asked in unison. 'Is there something wrong?'

'I don't know why, but I don't feel safe here,' she said uneasily.

Strange. The small stable was in fact rather

rundown, but we felt it would serve our purpose for one night. It was made of clay, and the floor was of fresh earth, which absorbed sounds and muffled our voices. Four wooden pallets covered with carpets and soft furs stood by the walls, and in the middle of the room was a large flat stone that served as a table. The monk placed the butter lamp on the stone and mumbled a couple of words before disappearing into the oncoming darkness.

Sitting in silence on our pallets, we listened to the night. Outside, it was strangely quiet; not a sound from the nearby village, no rush of water, no wind, not even the scratching of rats' feet. The utter silence actually made us begin to feel uneasy and apprehensive, but none of us had the courage to crawl under the fur and try to get some sleep.

'What a beautiful day it was!' Biria said, trying to make conversation. But her voice sounded too loud, somehow unnatural.

'Yes,' I answered, 'what a fascinating experience!' The carpet covering my pallet felt cool and clammy. All I wanted to do was sit there for a while and let exhaustion take over.

Dolma, crouching close beside me, had pulled the fur up over her shoulders. Up to now, she hadn't said a word. At one point she half whispered that she had to go to the bathroom but didn't dare venture out into the dark alone. The bathroom was located on some rocks behind the hut. First you had to circle the rocks, find the wooden ladder, then climb up ten wobbly steps.

'What in the world are you afraid of?' Biria wanted to know. 'Ghosts? There aren't any ghosts. They only exist in fairy tales.' She obviously was trying to sound detached and amused, but without much success.

Finally I gathered up my courage. 'Come on, Dolma, I'll be glad to go with you. As you know, I can get around perfectly well in the dark!'

'No, no,' Dolma replied, 'you wouldn't know how to escape them.'

'Escape *who*?' I asked, trying to sound casual in spite of my goose bumps.

'I mean the *dres*. There are hundreds of them here.' And she told us the story of the Khampas who were murdered during the Tibetan war of independence while trying unsuccessfully to defend a bridge against the Chinese. According to Tibetan belief, these murdered souls live on as *dres* — demons.

I remembered the old stone bridge, which led to the place where we had left our horses behind with Pola. We had ridden beneath it that morning, and Dolma had begged us to remain completely silent so that the ghosts wouldn't notice us. Under the beautiful morning sun, ghosts had seemed totally absurd to us. Biria and I had started to poke fun of Dolma, but we noticed that not only she, but Pola too, was becoming increasingly quiet and serious as we approached the bridge, so we decided to cease and desist: no more attempted jokes. And the demons were soon forgotten. The sun was shining, the river was merrily gurgling along beside our path, and the horses were trotting livelier than ever.

But now, in the dark of night, those *dres* were fast becoming a threatening presence. Nevertheless, Biria and I stoutly refused to own up to our growing apprehension. Dolma stood up, took the butter lamp in her hand, went over to one of the windows, and listened. 'They're not far,' she said. 'It's better for me to go alone. I have some experience with *dres*.' She opened the door as quietly as possible and disappeared with the lamp, leaving us in complete darkness.

'Do you believe in ghosts?' I asked Biria.

'Nonsense!' she answered quietly, moving closer to me on the pallet, 'You know it's all just superstition.'

'But the Tibetans do believe in *dres*,' I ventured, remembering all the classical texts about demons I had had to translate back at the university, texts that told of special people capable of feeling the presence of the *dres*, of hearing them, even seeing and making contact with them.

I told Biria everything I knew about *dres*. She just laughed. 'You're acting as if you of all people believed in this nonsense,' she said reprovingly.

'Of course I don't believe in ghosts,' I said angrily, nudging her off my pallet and crawling under my furs.

At length Dolma returned to the hut, slipping inside and closing the door gently behind her, doing her best to make sure it made no noise. She appeared exhausted. During her flight home, she said, she had lost the butter lamp. 'But I found you!' she managed, apparently greatly relieved.

'Was someone following you?' Biria asked, both curious and a trifle provocative.

'I don't know,' Dolma sighed, 'I simply zigzagged my way back, and *they* lost my tracks.'

I remembered a text about the *dres* that explained they can only move in a straight line — that is, they can't turn corners — a belief shared throughout Asia. That explains why there are so-called ghost walls in front of doors that prevent anyone — or anything — from making a beeline to the entrance of a house. When I had first heard of the *dres'* Achilles' heel — the fact that these poor demons couldn't navigate around corners — I found it rather funny. Tonight, however, I caught myself being comforted by the knowledge that my bed was not in a direct line from the window. Any *dres* that might make their way into the hut could never reach me. With that thought in mind, I snuggled down beneath the furs and soon fell fast asleep.

* * *

Sometime late in the night I woke up with a start. Something here *was* different. I propped myself up on my elbows and for a long time listened to the night, trying to figure out what it was that was sending a cold chill down my spine. Biria was snoring quietly under her furs. No sound came from Dolma's pallet. Perhaps like me, she too was sitting up stock-still, listening to the night. I heard a noise at the door — a little scratching at first, then a faint hissing, and finally a soft creak, as if someone was trying to break in. Can ghosts open doors? I asked myself, against all common sense. Still, my palms were sweating.

Something was stirring. I heard a constant

107

rustling in front of the door, a scratching against the clay walls, and a quiet but slowly rising drumming sound on the ground around the hut.

'Dolma, what's going on?' I whispered fearfully.

'They're trying to get into the hut,' came the answer from her pallet.

'What do they have against us?' Bloody images flashed through my mind. I imagined I saw long shadowy forms moving back and forth on the other side of the window, shoving blood-encrusted Khampa daggers into the room.

'Once they took my uncle,' Dolma whispered. 'When we found him again, he was a long, long way from home. His mind was affected. To this day he can't think straight.'

I shuddered and instinctively grabbed my pallet. 'But what do they want from us, of all people?' I asked in the darkness.

'We're strangers here. That must have attracted them.'

We remained silent for a long while, listening to what was taking place just outside. The drumming grew louder and louder, and soon we became aware of a quiet snuffling. Images of vampires came to mind, sticking their sniffing noses and shiny teeth through the window.

Dolma's pallet was directly beneath the window. Suddenly she threw off her furs, got up, and raced over to me, as if she could actually see what had been going through my terrified imagination. Trembling, she sat down beside me. Together we listened to the racket, expecting something incredible to burst in on us any minute.

Suddenly Dolma jumped up. 'The dogs are here now!' She sounded almost relieved.

I remembered from the Tibetan texts that *dres* are invisible to the human eye, but not to the canine. The dogs that now came racing in our direction, barking loudly, were clear evidence that the *dres* were really there.

'Now the dogs are here!' The world outside seemed to have been waiting for these words, for suddenly the night was filled with noise: a pack of village dogs was racing around our hut, howling and barking their lungs out.

The ruckus woke up Biria. 'What's going on?' she asked nervously.

'It's the dogs,' I answered curtly. I noticed that now she too looked worried, which gave me a tinge of satisfaction.

The three of us were sitting on the bed, listening intently to what was going on outside. Suddenly we stopped breathing. In spite of the mad dogs barking, we could hear slow, dragging steps coming closer and closer.

I felt my limbs stiffen. Even my tongue lay limp in my mouth, which was bone-dry. Muted by the buzzing in my ears, I heard Biria's worried voice: 'Aren't ghosts supposed to be afraid of dogs?'

I grabbed Dolma's arm and whispered, 'Dolma, who can that be? I thought you couldn't hear Khampa *dres*?'

'I don't know,' Dolma murmured. She sounded perplexed as we heard footsteps coming slowly but surely straight toward our hut. Not far from the door, the steps came to a halt. Instinctively we retreated to the farthest corner of the hut, where we cowered on the ground, crouching there for what seemed like an eternity, listening to our hearts beating so loudly they drowned out even the deafening noise the dogs were making. Then a deep male voice mumbled a long prayer, after which the dogs retreated to the village. Then everything grew quiet.

The door creaked open, and in came the old monk, holding in his hand the butter lamp that Dolma had lost during her escape from the demons. Sooner than you can say *dres*, we were all sitting on our pallets again. Had he seen us cowering on the floor? Biria and I were embarrassed by our panic attack, which now suddenly seemed totally unwarranted. What had really happened? Was this whole terrifying episode a figment of our imagination, or had indeed the *dres* come to visit us in the dead of night? Looking back, I'm still not sure.

11

It was midnight, and the Barkhor was in full swing. Guided to the Jokhand by the sound of whispered prayers and rotating prayer mills, as pilgrims do their *khora* — or evening rounds — I was able to make my way to the temple. The characteristic noise that the little wooden plates fastened to pilgrims' hands and knees make as they throw themselves onto the stone ground was an additional and helpful landmark for me.

I had arrived in front of the temple. The monk standing guard at the entrance took me gently by the arm, leading me to an inner courtyard. As soon as the monastery's heavy door closed behind me, the Barkhor din instantly subsided. I had entered another world. I marveled each time at the extraordinary contrast. None of the intrusive outside sounds — merchants yelling into megaphones, and the bass continuo of pilgrim's prayers — penetrated this sanctuary. The monastery had become my haven.

The familiar, pungent smell of melted butter emanating from lamps around the courtyard permeated the air, becoming almost suffocating. When total darkness set in, I was usually able to feel and detect these lamps. Keeping the lamps to my right, I did my own semi-*khora*, half circling the courtyard.

A draft — indicating another passage — led me to a second inner courtyard, where young monks had gathered in a cluster, waiting to enter the hall of prayers. Once we were inside the courtyard, the monks squired me to a place next to a column, where I took a seat on the cold stone floor. Soothed by the sweet and pungent butter smell, I began to relax, waiting for the evening prayer to start. My eyes, after many days under the harsh Tibetan sun, were tired, and I appreciated the pale light from the lamps, which had a healing effect. Even blind people, in their own way, are sensitive to light intensity.

In recent days I had made it a practice to come each evening at dusk to the Jokhand, seeking a moment of peace.

The main evening prayer in the monastery lasts one hour — from seven to eight — and the hundred or so participating monks chant psalms from the canon of Buddhist texts. I always looked forward to that hour. Now, having come at a later hour, I was taking full advantage of the peace, meditating on the past weeks' events.

Ever since my initial journey on horseback with Dolma and Biria, a whirlwind of events had given new momentum to our project. I badly needed this moment of silence to take stock and reflect. The monastery was the perfect place.

It had all started when Dolma and I visited an orphanage several days before. The director, a man named Lopsang, apparently eager to meet me, had asked Dolma to bring me over. He received us warmly in his elegant carpeted office. Separated from the entrance by a heavy curtain serving as door, his office seemed rather grand, even formal, with its lacquered desk on sculpted wooden legs. In one corner a big altar bore several statues of Buddha and precious silver filigree offering cups. A faint scent of incense added to the solemn atmosphere. At Lopsang's instigation, people suddenly appeared, carrying trays of pastries and fritters, which they passed around, together with sweet tea with milk. Unlike the salted butter tea offered by everyone from morning to night in Tibet, sweet tea is generally reserved for special occasions. Speaking directly in Tibetan with Dolma, Lopsang queried her intensely about me and our project: the new braille language in Tibetan I had devised. Dolma meticulously translated every detail of our project for him.

Seemingly impressed by what he heard, Lopsang was clicking his tongue — apparently a sign of approval in Tibet. We described for him our journey on horseback through the countryside in search of blind children, and told him how appalled we had been by the abject living conditions of so many of the blind children we had met.

'An institute for the blind is badly needed — in fact, long overdue,' we told him. 'Our goal is to start first with a grammar school, then later open a vocational school.'

It was a pleasant visit, more a social event, a public relations gesture, than anything else, we figured. But a few days later, an employee of the orphanage, a man named Palden, knocked on my door at the inn. 'The director wants to see you!' Palden said. 'Now!' he added. There was urgency in his voice.

Up till now I had depended on Dolma for all my business meetings. But this sudden urgency allowed me no time to go in search of her. I had no choice but to accept. Perched precariously on the back of Palden's bike, off I went to see Lopsang right then and there.

This time Lopsang received me in a big, impersonal, and chilly hall. Seated on an uncomfortable leather chair, I was offered salted tea. Judging from the sound as he tapped on the desk with his fingers, he was sitting across from me.

'I was delighted by my first visit with you,' I told him as a way to open dialogue, 'and I am honored to be here again!'

'Ohla-eh!' was his ambiguous answer.

I was beginning to be a little unsettled when the door opened and in came a third person. I heard Lopsang breathe a sigh of relief.

'My name is Chungda,' she said in perfect English. 'I am the director's daughter. My father asked that I help him interpret, as he only speaks Tibetan and Chinese.'

Chungda brought her chair closer, and her father began speaking.

'My father knows you've come here to help our needy citizens. He considers you a friend of Tibet, and has the highest respect for those who help the poor and the downtrodden.'

However flattering, this preamble seemed a bit stiff to me. Was this the way Tibetans always opened a discussion? I would have to wait and see.

'My father wishes to welcome you and thanks you for your dedication in the name of all Tibetans,' she went on.

Still finding all this rather excessive, I answered, 'Thank you, but until now, I don't feel I've really accomplished anything all that extraordinary.'

'Everyone in Lhasa knows you've come here to teach new writing to the blind. That's why my father insists on thanking you.'

How nice, I thought, but I couldn't help but wonder about the real reason Lopsang had sent for me so urgently. He had to have a different agenda.

Taking a deep breath, she continued, 'My father used to be a monk. For many years he dedicated his life to religion, until one day he suffered some terrible political problems. He was thrown into prison! These were difficult times for him, and for all of us.

'But finally Father was freed, on the condition he renounce all political activities. Called by his religious superior, he was given the mandate of bettering the life of his fellow Tibetans — by nonpolitical means only. With the help of some foreign friends, he founded this orphanage. We now have thirty pupils learning to read and write. We will offer vocational instruction as well later on.'

'We never received any official help from anyone here,' Lopsang added bitterly. 'No one seems interested in what we do for our country.'

Walking away from me and turning his back as if addressing an invisible audience, he continued in a voice that made everything sound quite dramatic. His daughter's translation, by contrast, was calm and sober.

'My father has known poverty in his life. Today he has vowed to give clothing, food, instruction, and affection to his orphans. His main goal is for them to embrace life with joy and appreciate it.'

Barely waiting for the translation to reach me, he walked back towards me and spoke again, his daughter's English following his Tibetan by a scant second or two.

'My father wants to make you an offer,' she intoned. 'He is so touched by what he has heard about you and your project, he wants to help open your school for the blind.'

I wasn't sure I had heard correctly. This offer was completely unexpected, especially in the context of the melodramatic scene I had previously witnessed. I turned to the director and managed to stutter, 'What an extraordinary and generous offer! How can I ever thank you!'

I was still searching for words in my confused head as Chungda went on: 'We are building a new extension to the orphanage. It's going to be quite large. My father proposes to let you share a big enough space to accommodate your needs for your school.'

A school? Real classrooms for the school? In this forsaken country where nothing ever works, how could such a miracle suddenly happen out of the blue? I had been fully prepared to fight the obstacle course of China's omnipresent bureaucracy. In Tibet or China, I had learned, no one listens, no one hears you. You can never get agreement about anything from anyone. Not that you ever get a clear-cut rejection either. Nothing is ever justified, or even explained, and no one in the bureaucratic maze is prepared to take responsibility. Passing the buck is the name of the game — a Kafka bureaucracy in its most refined form. Ultimately you end up dancing from one department to the other. Lopsang's direct, generous offer came to me as a great surprise — and a pleasant one.

Only a few days earlier, I reminded myself, I had presented my school project to an official at the municipal office, telling him my goal was to start an institution for the blind. I then proceeded to demonstrate in great detail the principles of the new language for the blind I had devised, explaining how I intended to teach braille in Tibetan. While I was in the official's office making my pitch, I could hear people from surrounding offices quietly huddling outside his door, listening in.

'How can a blind student, fresh from the West, operating alone without any official sanction, tackle such an endeavor?' asked the official sitting across from me.

Seizing the moment, and taking full advantage of the gathering audience outside his office — and mildly conscious that this might be the perfect and only moment to speak without reservation — I launched into an elaborate explanation of my school project. No government official ever gives the time of day to any private individual, I said, thanking him for hearing me out, saying I felt lucky to be sitting in his office. When my presentation was finished, all those hovering outside rushed in, thanking me and shaking my hand.

'You must first raise funds for the project. We'll take it from there,' responded the official, no doubt surprised at his own words and perhaps intimidated by his unexpected audience.

That meeting — still vivid in my mind — made Lopsang's spontaneous offer seem all the more extraordinary.

Thanking him again, I suggested we meet soon to review the terms of our future collaboration. Overcome with emotion, I returned to Banak Shol in a jeep ordered by Lopsang and rushed over to see Dolma.

'What a big heart that Lopsang has!' she said, clearly delighted by my news. 'Without question, you'll need a local partner to start your school, and Lopsang seems an excellent choice. It's important, though, to find out exactly how he views your collaboration. Be very careful, and make sure you examine every aspect of the situation before you enter into this partnership.'

In the following weeks, Lopsang and I met several times. Gone were the friendly and flowery words of our first encounter, along with the purple language of the second. Within a few days, I mobilized all my faculties in a crash course on the art of negotiation. It was imperative that I turn myself around and become an instant savvy tactician.

Lopsang's daughter took part in all our meetings. Somehow, they made it clear to me, though without quite articulating it, that Dolma was not welcome, which concerned me. But after each of our tedious and lengthy sessions — par for the course here, I knew — I would fill Dolma in. Finally, when all details of our deal seemed agreed upon, Lopsang and I, in the presence of witnesses, formally signed the provisional agreement. My role was to raise funds and be in charge of planning and organizing the project. His was to provide the space for the school for the blind.

We celebrated the signing by going out to a

restaurant, where much delicious food and *arka* — the local wine — was enjoyed by all.

★ ★ ★

The faint rustle of monks' robes and occasional discreet clearing of a throat interrupted the deep silence around me. A baritone voice began a prayer whose words I did not understand. Younger, higher voices followed. As the lower voice wove back in, many more voices joined the chorus. The chant rose in regular waves around three notes, before a gradual decrescendo brought it back to a murmur. At that point the sound of little bells, drums, and horns took over. It had a magical effect on me.

In perfect unison, the horns ascended until, reaching a high note, they slid back down. After all the instruments fell silent, prayers began again. The baritone voice reentered in a counterpoint with other voices, in different rhythms. Together with the instruments, they all sang faster and faster, until the rhythm reached a frenetic level. In this half-sung, half-spoken choir, I could identify a staccato of three and four beats. Then, one after the other, the many different voices fell out of the chorus, leaving the baritone dramatically alone to conclude the prayer.

This monotonous chant inevitably lulled me into a dreamlike state, but every now and then the sound of tiny tinkling bells and the drumbeat would pull me out of my reverie. This was my hour for reflecting and relaxing. No one knew me here. No one asked questions I didn't feel like answering. There were no derogatory comments made about me behind my back. In the fragrant darkness of this hall of prayers, I felt protected from inquisitive looks, and let myself be carried along by the music and the chants.

★ ★ ★

'Hello!' I heard someone say in my ear. The instruments were so loud that I couldn't recognize the voice. I felt the presence of someone sitting next to me on the stone floor but decided not to respond. When the instruments stopped playing, the voice went on, 'What serenity! This is so wonderfully relaxing!'

Still not answering, I edged slightly away from the voice. He — it was a male voice — moved closer to me and shamelessly prattled on for several more minutes, a tirade of banalities, the voice drowning out the monks'. Increasingly irritated by this unasked-for intrusion, I wondered who this uncouth person could be. Someone I'd met? I still couldn't pinpoint the voice. Then all of a sudden I realized it was Paul, the Dutch fellow I had met back at the Banak Shol. Overcome by a slight pang of guilt at my standoffishness, I probably overcompensated with a greeting that was too effusive.

'Paul! Where in the world have you been these past few weeks?' I asked. 'And what are you doing here?'

'Volunteer work with the Red Cross. Next year, I'll get a contract as foreman with the Red Cross in Shigatse.'

Paul had told us he was going to try to find a job so he could stay in Tibet. Enterprising fellow. So he had succeeded! Whenever he had mentioned his plans, fellow tourists would shake their heads much as they did whenever I went on about my own project. 'You seem to forget,' they kept saying, 'only foreigners with fat wallets are welcome as tourists here. And besides, you can't get a work permit unless you belong to some influential humanitarian organization.'

Neither Paul nor I had paid any attention to these dire predictions. And, as it turns out, in both cases that attitude served us well. Apart from being a nonstop loud-mouth, if a nice one, Paul was known as a party animator. He was also a gifted jack-of-all-trades, always ready and willing to add a helping hand to any kind of building or fixing, you name it. It was no surprise he had been able to find work in Tibet.

I brought him up-to-date on my project.

'That's great! When will the school start?'

'That's the big question. It'll take months to raise funds. Then — '

'So we'll be here together next year! If you need me for bookkeeping, computer, or anything else, feel free to call on me!'

His boundless energy was already making me tired.

'Thank you, but we aren't there yet.'

'Call me when you know when you'll be returning to Tibet.'

'I will,' I promised.

Leaning against the column, I closed my eyes. The past weeks' negotiations had worn me out. I felt a slight knot in my stomach. Was I homesick? I let myself dream about a life with a modicum of security, rules one could rely on for a change, and perhaps simply a warm shower. The incense was making me nauseous and dizzy.

'Would you like some Coca-Cola?' Paul asked, his voice again too loud.

Not really an appropriate beverage for a holy place, I remarked to myself. But the air, heavy with smoke from the oil lamps, made me welcome the refreshing drink. If only Paul would stop making so much racket as he scoured his bag for the elusive can of Coke.

'Shh!' I admonished him. This was the moment when monks meditate in total silence. Time seemed to have stopped. I held my breath, aware that any small sound here resonates like a clanging cymbal. Paul had finally found the can, but his noisy rummaging was completely unnerving. For God's sake — no, for Buddha's sake! — I begged him to stop.

Now another problem surfaced: he couldn't open the can! When finally he did, it sounded as if all the demons were escaping at once. The warm monastery, plus the fact that Paul had been carrying the Coke on his back all day, had rendered the can doubly effervescent. The spray gushed upward, hit the ceiling, and cascaded slowly back down onto the statues and the holy assembly.

I was refreshed. And duly mortified.

12

On my return to Germany to raise money for the school, Elmar, a friend of mine, helped me compose the following press release, which we sent out to all the papers and news agencies.

August 14, 1997

From May until August 1997, Sabriye Tenberken, a twenty-six-year-old student in Tibetan studies at the University of Bonn, has traveled through the Tibet Autonomous Region in order to collect data and investigate the condition of the blind.

According to official sources, there are more than 10,000 blind people in Tibet, of which many are school-age children. The principal cause for the eye lesions are the powerful sun rays, the dust, soot from the houses, and generally a lack of medical infrastructure.

Blind children in Tibet have no access to any form of education, and no possibility of social integration. Too many blind children are locked up in dark huts — their ashamed parents hide them from the neighbors. Others, from an early age, are forced to beg in the street. Many are often virtually abandoned by their family. In the course of her trip on horseback, the student even discovered a four-year-old girl tied to her bed because her parents, working in the fields, were concerned that, if left alone, she might hurt herself.

Before going to Tibet, Sabriye Tenberken had devised a version of braille in Tibetan. During her trip to Asia, she contacted the authorities and requested permission to start a pilot school, whose mission was to teach blind children braille, as well as other techniques of orientation necessary to live an independent life.

The school is scheduled to open in April of next year. Eight children — from the age of seven to thirteen — are already registered for the school.

The space for Miss Tenberken's school has been provided by an orphanage in Lhasa. In the early years, Sabriye herself intends to teach while training teachers who will carry on for her later.

One of Miss Tenberken's objectives is

to reintegrate blind children into their village schools, where she also plans to send the teachers she has trained.

Sabriye Tenberken is currently fundraising for her school for the blind in Germany as well as in the rest of Europe.

'If you want to raise funds for your school,' Elmar said, 'you need to be known. You must *sell* your idea.'

Most newspapers who picked up on the story opted for a tabloid approach, and that didn't help the cause.

'A BLIND STUDENT CROSSES TIBETAN PLAIN ON HORSEBACK,' read the headline, or 'A BLIND GERMAN GIRL PULLS BLIND TIBETAN CHILDREN FROM THEIR DARK HOME. She brings them light, and the writing she teaches them opens the door to a better life for them.'

Only a few papers emphasized the fundraising aspect. One correspondent called me to say, 'Frankly, Sabriye, we don't believe your story!'

★　★　★

'Don't count on the press,' advised another friend. 'You have to try to get subsidies from government organizations, even if it's only

129

seed money. The rest will follow.'

At the Ministry for Economic Cooperation and at Help for Development, I was informed that only those sponsored by an association for public works could apply for financial aid.

'Fine,' I replied. 'How long does it take to form such an association?'

'No, no.' The man laughed. 'You must be sponsored by an *existing* association. One that has been functioning for at least five years.'

I swallowed hard. How in the world was I supposed to find such an organization in the few weeks I was in Germany?

It seemed tricky, to say the least. Maybe even hopeless.

★ ★ ★

As fate would have it, a few days later I met through some friends a woman who was the head of an existing organization, and was not only interested but anxious to help. Over cakes and fruit juice, the president of 'my' new association and I met on a sunny terrace in the center of town to discuss our new partnership. Seven years earlier she had founded her association to help integrate handicapped Chinese into the mainstream of society. Till now she had managed to raise a fair amount of money, but lately people were increasingly reluctant to make substantial donations. Money was drying up, she told me, shaking her head.

Still, she seemed optimistic about my project, and was looking forward to meeting and working with new blood. I was invited the next day to a board meeting of her association, where she introduced me to its members. It was a positive afternoon. Everyone at the board meeting seemed cordial and truly interested in the fate of blind children. I gave them details of my agreement with Lopsang and left the meeting feeling good.

Subsequently I was interviewed on German television. My project was the center of the show, and as a result several schools, universities, and clubs invited me to lecture. There were even raffles and silent auctions, whose profits went directly to our school. I was of course pleased as punch.

While I had the impression that things were moving forward reasonably well, to my surprise, important organizations such as the Federation for the Blind and Relief Organizations for Tibet appeared reticent. I'm convinced that in the eyes of these two politically pro-Tibet official organizations — both of which I went to see — I must have seemed hopelessly naive.

'All the money we send to Tibet is intercepted by the Chinese,' they explained. 'We know it never arrives to help their cause for independence!'

'That's not really what I'm interested in,' I replied. 'What I want is to find a way to educate and help blind people integrate themselves into society.'

Since my return home from Tibet, what most shocked me was the apparent lack of interest these supposedly 'do-good' organizations showed in the blind.

'Why should we worry about the Tibetan blind?' said a blind man eating a mammoth steak, with whom I had struck up a conversation in a brasserie where I was lunching one day. 'We need to help our own blind.'

'What do you mean?' I asked.

'Let's start with traffic lights. They should be replaced by sonic devices.'

'Absolutely, Hanz!' echoed his wife, 'Not to mention the need to install a loudspeaker in every bus announcing the station well before the bus arrives there, so blind passengers have plenty of time to get out. That's the kind of thing they need!'

In the course of my stay, I heard many such remarks but always took them in stride. Still,

132

I was very touched by the unexpected support so many people back home showed for my project. Some went so far as to turn down gifts for their anniversaries, birthdays, or weddings, asking instead that a donation be made to our school.

In the meantime, the 'sponsoring association' that had agreed to take me on remained increasingly — and disturbingly — silent. Not having heard from the association's founder, the woman with whom I had had coffee a couple of weeks before, I gave her a call.

'Your project is of course your main concern, Sabriye,' she told me on the phone, 'but you must understand that our organization is involved in many such projects. Besides, I'm a single mother. My hands are more than full.' Nonetheless, she agreed to let me go ahead if I were to provide all or most of the back-office effort, noting that her responsibilities would have to be confined to signing official documents needed along the way. She thanked me for my understanding. So much for my new association, which I could feel was already fast receding into the woodwork.

At the recommendation of the association's president, I met with the Department of Education. I found some encouragement there; people reacted positively to my pitch about the school, but they voiced one major concern: my sponsoring association. 'In our opinion,' they said, 'it's not a sufficiently professional group. You need a more competent sponsoring agent.'

I promised to look for another association. Before I had a chance to do so, however, I received the good news that my present association had approved my request for seed money. I must have made a convincing presentation that day at their board meeting. In any event, that grant, together with the various gifts and donations already received, meant that in less than six months after my return to Germany, I had collected all the funding necessary to start my school. All I needed now was an official invitation from Lopsang — and a work permit. I called Lopsang in Lhasa, and two months later — things do take their little time in Asia — the documents finally arrived.

With my plane ticket for Kathmandu in hand, I was ready to go on my big mission! At long last my dream was becoming a reality.

I made my rounds, saying good-bye to everyone I knew in Germany, thanking all those who had made my dream come true. I checked my address book one last time to make sure no one had been left out. Oh, yes: Paul Kronenberg! I remembered my promise to call him when I was ready to return to Tibet.

'Hello, Paul! I just wanted to say good-bye and let you know I'm returning to Lhasa next week.'

'You are?' he asked laconically.

I was surprised that was all the reaction my news had triggered. At least he could have wished me bon voyage! I thought.

After a silence that seemed interminable, he said, 'What do you mean, telling me good-bye? Tomorrow I'm quitting my job. I'm coming with you!'

13

'Ladies and gentlemen, in a few moments you will see on your left Mount Everest, the highest mountain in the world.'

That was the moment the passengers had all been waiting for. Rushing to the left side of the plane, they all pressed their heads against the windows.

As for me, I remained seated on the right side of the plane, feeling that, all on my own, I was keeping the plane in balance.

'Do you realize how lucky we are?' Paul exclaimed, sitting back down beside me. 'We're free to decide what we want to do with our lives.'

Immediately after my farewell phone call to him from Germany, he had, true to his word, handed in his resignation as coordinator of a Dutch amusement park where for the past year he had been responsible for dealing with an endless stream of customer complaints. During those twelve long months, he had addressed and processed some twenty-two thousand complaints. Enough was enough. He was more than happy to leave all this negative work behind and come back to Tibet with me.

'There are more important things in life,' he told me. 'I believe in your school. I want to help you. I can help build the school, install computers, be useful in all sorts of different ways.'

★   ★   ★

'Kelsang Meto! Here you are at last! We expected you last week!' a shrill voice hailed me soon after I had arrived in Lhasa.

It was Chungda, who, unannounced, had entered my room, doubtless thinking the day after my arrival I would jump out of bed and start working immediately.

I hated her to see me looking so unkempt. Besides, I was in a state of total exhaustion and needed to get my bearings. For six long days we had been stuck in Kathmandu, and the night before, the steep climb from 6,000 to 12,000 feet had made me ill. I was still suffering from acute migraine.

'The chauffeur is waiting downstairs,' Chungda continued excitedly. 'We can't wait to show you the school! It's ready to open!'

'I'll be right there,' I said, praying for her to leave me alone.

'I'll help you.' And she started rummaging in my open suitcase. Was she trying to help me get dressed?

'Please, give me five minutes. I'll be right down.'

With a cold towel spread against my forehead, I climbed into Lopsang's jeep, on my way to my new school. Chungda's incessant chatter didn't help my migraine.

'We're so happy you've arrived. Father went to the airport three times last week. We thought you'd never come back!'

'I'm sorry. I missed my connection in Kathmandu.'

The orphanage's new buildings were at the other end of town. Because of the bad roads, it took forever to get there. Lopsang was standing at the entrance, waiting for us. After the initial amenities, exchange of presents, and some salted buttered tea, we went straight to his new office. 'My' school was across from the orphanage. Lopsang couldn't wait to take me there.

Through the window I could hear children reciting the Tibetan alphabet. Elsewhere, the scream of electric saws and the pounding of hammers could be heard. A group of children rushed up to us with questions.

'This is Kelsang Meto. She is going to teach your blind schoolmates,' explained Chungda. They all followed us, as if behind the pied piper, through the courtyard.

'Here is your school. It has two levels. The classroom, dining room, and toilets are downstairs.'

We entered a large, square, high-ceilinged room. All this empty space seemed slightly unwelcoming at first, but I figured it would be fine when it was furnished.

After climbing a staircase, we emerged onto a landing with a balcony that led us to three dormitories, two staff rooms, and a shower room.

'So luxurious!' I remarked. Lopsang and Chungda responded with a satisfied chuckle.

What will happen to these poor children who, till now, have known only utter misery? I wondered. After living this princely life, will they ever want to go back to their village huts?

We crossed the courtyard and entered another building.

'Here we've installed your school's offices,' Chungda announced proudly.

As we went up one flight of stairs, we entered a large room with unfamiliar echoes.

'This room is five hundred square feet,' Chungda announced proudly. 'The floor is entirely covered by thick carpeting. On your left, windows looking onto the courtyard. On your right, trees. We can see all the way to Potala. If you want to impress people, here is where you should bring them.'

I tried to orient myself by walking all the way around the room. It was huge and empty, except for a table and a few chairs. I found it oppressive. Chungda led me through a door into another room.

'Here's your office! With two desks!' she said.

'I thought we had agreed last year that we would pick furniture together!' I said, trying to conceal my disappointment.

'We took care of everything.'

'Everything? Tables, chairs, benches, mattresses, sheets, plates, cutlery?'

'Yes. And we kept strictly to budget!' she continued, obviously pleased.

The money for all that was to be wire-transferred from Germany after my return to Lhasa. Before I went back to Germany eight months before, Chungda and I had established a list of necessary items and agreed to do the shopping together upon my return. Although I realized that she had saved me considerable time and effort, I couldn't help but be taken aback at not having participated in furnishing my school.

'Shopkeepers here tend to take advantage of foreigners,' Chungda said, sensing my disappointment. 'Why pay more than you have to? Save your donation money for your blind.'

Our anticipated budget to furnish the school was eleven thousand marks — a fortune in terms of Tibet's living standards. 'Where did you find the money for all that?' I asked Chungda.

'My father and I loaned you the money, knowing there would soon be money transferred from Germany to our account.'

I too was expecting and looking forward to receiving the transfer from my sponsoring association. My migraine was coming back, and I started walking slowly around the room.

'Aren't you pleased?' asked Chungda, with a hint of trepidation in her voice.

'Oh, yes. I just wasn't expecting a place this big.'

'It's also light, airy, and impeccably clean. The building was finished this winter. Very modern, built in concrete.'

We walked over to the residential part. I could move in immediately, she said. Both the ground floor and the first story had a modern bathroom and three bedrooms. In the back, a terrace led to a garden. As we walked outside, Chungda identified the plants and the trees, all in bloom.

I called Paul immediately.

'You won't need to help me build my school. It's all done,' I told him.

'And how are the buildings?'

'Handsome. And very spacious.' I could not remember the precise topography. It would take a bit more time and exploration to make a real impression on me. 'It's hard to say. There is no atmosphere yet. But after it's furnished, I'm sure it'll change.'

The buildings — so generously offered by Lopsang — I had to admit, were indeed sumptuous. Whenever I dreamed of building my school in Tibet, I certainly never imagined such luxury. I couldn't remember what I had been expecting? Huts made of mud? Stables? A tent made of yak skin?

In a modern city like Lhasa, why not have buildings made of concrete? On the other hand, Tibet is a country with blazing hot summers and icy cold winters, and concrete doesn't protect against the cold the way traditional Tibetan huts do. But there it was — all finished and ready for me to start. I was overwhelmed, slightly intimidated by the newness of it all.

Seated on a low wall in the garden, I listened with utter delight to the birds chirping and the buzzing of bees, and breathed in the intense perfume of the flowers. I had landed in paradise! Lopsang and Chungda had outdone themselves in every respect, including making me feel at home in this castle. I was fully aware that, thanks to them both, my dream — the school for the blind — had now become a reality.

By early June, I had picked one of the ground-floor rooms as mine and settled into my new home. The voices of children reading ancient texts filtering through the classroom windows of the orphanage on the other side of the courtyard were a welcome background sound. Sweet innocent voices, rising and falling in a rhythm a little like that of the Jokhang — the orphans' ritual evening prayer — would become my daily background music.

I was the sole occupant of this residence — Paul was in Shigatse, five hundred miles from Lhasa, on Red Cross business — and I found myself often jolted by the unfamiliar sounds all around: screeching doors, banging shutters, slamming windows, and even occasional footsteps on the terrace that kept me awake a good deal of the time. Each night I tried to reassure myself and dispel my fears, reminding myself that Lopsang had made it a kind of fortress, installing solid screens on the windows.

In the middle of my first night, a loud noise from the hallway woke me up. Unafraid, I opened the door, only to find myself deep in several inches of cold water. A water pipe had burst.

'It's always the same here,' Paul had warned me earlier on. 'On the surface everything looks impeccable. Up close you find the roof leaking, and if one coughs a little, the tiles quietly peel off the bathroom walls, revealing pipes that have turned rusty even before you had a chance to use them.'

I remained frozen, transfixed at the threshold of my room as water silently poured in. The old janitor, roused out of his sleep, ran to warn the other employees, who rushed to shut off the water main. Our poor orphans were shaken out of their beds and given buckets and big sponges. Like sleepy little robots, they were immediately put to work mopping up the water.

After that incident, not a single drop of running water was ever seen again in my luxurious bathroom! From then on, I had to cross the courtyard every morning with a bucket and bring water from the well up to the bathroom. In a way, that little daily ritual reassured me, reminding me I was in Tibet, a place I wanted to be.

14

One morning I set off with the intention of exploring how to get by foot to old Lhasa. No sooner had I reached the main door than a scream stopped me. Someone was holding me by the arm.

'What's going on?' I asked in Tibetan.

All shaken, the old janitor told me I had no right to go out on my own.

'Why?' I asked.

Before he had a chance to answer, Chungda appeared.

'You wish to go to town? Wait a minute, I'll get the chauffeur.'

'I much prefer to walk. The whole point of this exercise is for me to know the way.'

'That's impossible,' Chungda declared. 'My father strictly forbids it.'

I explained to Lopsang, who had also appeared on the scene, that as future head of a school for the blind it was imperative he started trusting blind people, and that began with trusting me.

'Don't worry about me,' I insisted. I could tell Chungda was quite irritated.

'To old Lhasa is straight ahead, right? Give

me a chance. I promise I'll come back safe and sound.'

Tired of fighting me, they gave up, opened the gate, and let me go. I made it to the center of town without any difficulty. At the first crossroad I ran by chance into a band of boys, who cheerfully escorted me to the Potala park and helped me into a bike-taxi. By chance? I had the distinct feeling that somehow Lopsang was behind this little maneuver. Despite my initial impatience with their overprotective attitude, I had to confess it touched me to know they cared so much.

I spent a wonderful afternoon with Dolma, and we decided to have dinner together. When it came time for me to go home, I yielded to Dolma's plea that I take a taxi back to the school.

'Do you know where the school is?' I asked my driver in Chinese.

'Of course I do! I was born in Lhasa. I know this town inside out.'

As luck would have it, he turned out to be not only ignorant but stupid. He also wouldn't believe me when I told him I was blind.

'Your eyes are moving! How many fingers am I holding up?'

'Fifteen, of course!' He burst out laughing. I had been through that little scenario many times before in my life.

After we crossed a bridge — I recognized by the sound the car made going over it — I asked him to stop and let me off. 'I know my way from this point on.' I couldn't wait to get out and walk.

'No! There is no way I'll let you get out, blind as you are!'

And he pushed down harder on the gas. I thought I recognized the smell of a dump close to the school, and asked a second time to get off.

'There's no school here!' he said. I realized he had no idea where we were, and at this point I didn't either. He continued driving on into the night, until he arrived at a gate. Driving through, inside the courtyard, he stopped the taxi. We were soon surrounded by giggling women. Who were they, I wondered? There was no mistake: we had arrived at a brothel.

'Do you know this woman?' he asked them. They went on giggling. 'Do you have any idea where she wants to go?'

I was getting seriously angry and gave him a piece of my mind.

'I know perfectly well where I want to go. Turn around, and follow my instructions from now on.'

After a short while, clearly weary of driving

me around, he stopped suddenly and in a loud voice announced, 'Here we are!'

I knew he was lying, but tired of this unnecessary merry-go-round, I handed him ten yuan — the usual fare for a taxi — and stepped out, slamming the door.

'Wait a minute!' he yelled. 'That's not enough!'

'It absolutely is. You have been completely incapable of finding the way, and because of you I'm now obliged to walk home alone. Thanks very much!'

He carried on with his inane histrionics, and to boot grabbed hold of my cane, preventing me from walking forward. I wrenched it free with all my strength and marched doggedly into the night. Treading through an almost unmanageable road riddled with puddles and garbage strewn along the way, my cane bumped against a steel pipe. It signaled a familiar landmark. I was relieved to recognize the city's outskirts. I had spotted that pipe earlier that afternoon. I breathed a sigh of relief; I was almost there!

I followed the long alley leading to our door and pounded on the door. To my great astonishment, it opened immediately. All the orphanage employees, worried sick about me and my long absence, were huddled together behind the gate. When they saw me, in a chorus they all expressed relief to see me back safe and sound.

'What happened to you? So late?'

'Oh, not much really. You really shouldn't have worried about me!' I casually pretended things were just fine.

Thanking them for their concern and using fatigue as an excuse, I went to my room. Only then, in the privacy of my own walls, did I admit to myself how scary it all could have been. Anxious to tell Paul about my latest adventure, I called him.

I was in the throes of imitating my chauffeur to Paul when I heard footsteps climbing the stairs. I stopped talking and listened attentively. The stranger had just reached the landing and was about to enter the living room. He was pushing the door open.

'What's going on?' Paul was yelling on the phone. 'Why aren't you speaking?'

I brought the phone close to my mouth and whispered, 'I'll call you back later. There's someone in the house; I don't know who.'

Silently I hung up, grabbed hold of my cane, and turned around. The only thing now separating me from the stranger was the door of the office, which had been left ajar. There were no lights on. As always, I felt more secure in darkness; this said, the presence of this stranger represented a menace, and I was getting worried. Unable to contain myself any longer, I asked in a tense voice, 'Who are you, and what do you want?'

I could hear him nervously shifting from one foot to the other. Then, all of a sudden, a torrent of words poured forth — none of which made any sense to me. I couldn't understand a word. It was neither Tibetan nor Chinese. Could it be my irate taxi driver coming to collect what he thought I owed him? I finally realized he was speaking some broken English. It could only be Palden, one of the orphanage teachers. Like all the others, he had been sincerely worried about me and had come to assure himself that everything was all right. Immensely relieved, I put down my cane and sat on my desk. I knew he wouldn't leave until he had heard the details of my night adventure, so I filled him in.

'How in the world did you find your way back?' Palden asked.

'Thanks to my good old cane,' I replied, putting the cane in his hands. 'Close your eyes, and try navigating with it.'

Palden turned out to be a talented student. Observing him was both funny and instructive. We laughed a lot together. After turning clumsily round and round, it took him no time at all to learn how to stop bumping into furniture, how deftly to avoid it. We spent a full hour with this exercise, and only then, to my utter consternation, did I remember that Paul was waiting by the phone for me to call back.

A few days later, Palden came back to see me. He was interested to know where I stood with my project.

At that time, I needed to hire teachers for the school and had begun interviewing. Finding qualified people eager to work, people with what I considered two indispensable attributes — namely, an elementary knowledge of English and a good level of Chinese — but more importantly, intuitively capable of putting themselves inside the mind of a blind person, was trickier than I had thought. I had devised a test aimed not so much at testing their linguistic knowledge as at challenging their ability to orient themselves in total obscurity. Palden's job was to select candidates who by word of mouth had heard about our interviews, and congregated in the courtyard. I had given him a bag of soft cloth blindfolds I had collected from my various airline flights, and he was to fit them on the candidates. One by one he brought them up to me, and I asked them to orient themselves blindfolded in their new environment. Most would start by stumbling, turning around aimlessly. I would then suggest they find a landmark that would help them systematically explore the new space.

Those who picked the table in the middle of the room as a starting point learned to let their hands follow its contours. When that didn't seem to help, they ended up circling the table, remaining close to it. Others, a bit more adventurous, would hug the walls, for doing so would give them a quick, general sense of the space. Standing by the door, I spoke to them while they were exploring, hoping the sound of my voice would give them a better sense of the place as well as their position within it. Whenever I heard someone bumping against a bookcase filled with books somewhere in the room, I would explain that, to avoid this, it would be a good idea to walk with hands extended in front. As soon as candidates became more familiar with the space and felt comfortable enough to move away from the walls, they ventured forth, crossing the room without relying on any further landmark. During those sessions, many were felled by vertigo. Others expressed wonderment at being able to orient themselves with the help of the slightest noise or echo as landmark, or even a mere fluctuation in temperature.

During one of those sessions, a young Tibetan girl managed to get all tangled up with a box that was filled with newspapers and wrapping paper. I rushed to her rescue, liberating her from her paper prison.

'This job is for me! I've never had such fun! Ever!'

Her name was Anila. She had been a nun in a Lhasa convent. I liked her immediately. The problem, however, was that she could neither read nor write, and spoke neither English nor Chinese. Therefore I couldn't hire her as a teacher! Anila — the name given to all nuns in Tibet — was nonetheless hired as our school's manager, or 'house mother.' To this day, I consider her the best 'innkeeper' in the world.

But most of those I interviewed ended up panicky and tore their blindfolds off. Being afraid of not seeing was not a good beginning, I thought. I needed people able to relate fully to blind people. Only from that important starting point would anyone be able to discover the capabilities and limitations of each child and become a qualified teacher to the blind. To teach joy, self-confidence, and courage in daily life, teachers had to possess those qualities themselves.

Palden seemed alert and enthusiastic. The

problem was, he was Lopsang's employee. There was no way I could or would steal him from the orphanage. I concentrated mainly on Lagpar, who had proved the most qualified candidate up to now. Lagpar was the director of a local hotel and earned a good living, but he was fed up with his job, he explained.

'I really don't enjoy my work anymore,' he said. 'I'd much rather work with children, even at a lower salary.' He appeared quite creative and learned more quickly than any of the candidates how to navigate without seeing, with the help of a cane. Wearing the cloth blindfold, he nonetheless moved like a streak of light, exploring the courtyard and all the buildings with great ease and speed. The orphans were having great fun stationing themselves along his route, giving him wrong directions and giggling in chorus when their false information led him into trouble.

I had decided to hire Lagpar. But alas, he wrote me a letter explaining that resigning from his position had proved impossible. I was terribly disappointed, and more than a little panicked. My first school session was around the corner, and now I had no teacher!

I shared my problem with Palden, who came each day to visit and chat. To my surprise, he told me that Lopsang wasn't particularly anxious to keep him. I found that hard to understand, since Palden seemed to me such a fine teacher. Each time I had the opportunity to observe his class, he had demonstrated total control of his thirty pupils — no easy task, given their different ages and personalities — while igniting their interest in whatever subject he was teaching. Most other teachers could only manage to maintain discipline by walking between each row of pupils and shaking the unruly ones, or even at times slapping them soundly, a practice I deplored. Palden's patience, on the other hand, was exemplary.

'I earn only two hundred yuan a month,' he confessed. 'Barely enough to pay my food and rent.' He was more and more embarrassed. 'When I asked for a raise, Lopsang lost his temper and suggested I leave. He would not try to keep me, he told me!'

The anticipated and budgeted salary for teachers in our school was much higher than that of a regular teacher: no less than a thousand yuan. When I told Chungda of my desire to hire Palden — only if they felt no conflict about it — she reassured me that it would pose no problem. I was thrilled.

Always formal, Lopsang asked that I give him time to think about it. If he were to agree, it would be with some conditions

— Palden would have to give a few teaching hours a week to the orphanage. It would be up to him, Lopsang, to decide how many hours and when. Salaries for our school would be managed by Chungda, and Lopsang would hand out salaries to all teachers. Without thinking of the possible consequences that arrogance might entail, I agreed.

Thus Palden became the first teacher in our institute for the blind in Tibet.

15

'Kelsang Meto! I've been looking for you. Where in the world have you been? We have distinguished visitors from Beijing who want to meet you!'

Chungda was out of breath from searching high and low to find me. That morning I had been working in the small dormitory. With the help of Anila and Palden, I was finishing screwing on the metal sides of the children's bunk beds. Of all mornings this was most certainly not the one to have unannounced visitors! With grease spots on my T-shirt and my hair dusty from the morning's work with saw and hammer, I was definitely not in any shape to meet distinguished guests.

'I'll run home and quickly change into something decent. Be right back!' I never got very far. Lopsang caught up with me in the stairway and, taking hold of my arm, led me down a few steps. There, willy-nilly, I found myself being introduced to the 'distinguished gentlemen.' They were delegates from the China Disabled Persons' Federation (CDPF). On a mission from Beijing to inspect the autonomous region of Tibet, they had heard of my school and were eager to meet me. I felt immediate tension overcome me. During my first trip to Beijing I had approached this organization, known for its remarkable work in central China, hoping that it would consider my project in Tibet desirable and manageable and endorse it.

I was told in no uncertain terms that the autonomous region of Tibet represented no priority for the federation, and absolutely no plans would be made for the Tibetan blind before 2007. The influence of the CDPF, whose head was Deng Pufang — son of former Chinese leader Deng Xiaoping — was getting stronger all the time, and had become very important in China.

During the Cultural Revolution, Deng Pufang was thrown out of a window; terribly wounded, he would spend the rest of his life in a wheelchair. He has since become the strongest and most efficient advocate in the fight for handicapped people's rights in China. In the space of a few years, his organization accomplished exemplary results. Thanks to Deng Pufang's efforts, doors still closed up to then — the stuff of utopian dreams for most countries — have opened for Chinese handicapped. Some professions have even been reserved specifically for the handicapped. For instance, in China, professional, medical, and physiotherapy masseuses are for the most part the blind or deaf. Those with eyesight or normal hearing who wish to practice these professions must obtain special permission. Since the early 1990s many new laws ensure and guarantee blind people's salaries, as well as promoting their social status in China.

The visitors' first question to me was why I had chosen Tibet rather than any other Chinese province. I had often been asked that very question by Chinese functionaries. They were perennially suspicious and paranoid about any European or North American who came to Tibet, sure it was for political reasons only. I hastened to explain that my choice had been a matter of chance, and proceeded to deliver a little speech I had memorized in Chinese, precisely for such occasions: 'Tibetan was my major at the Institute for Central Asian Languages and Cultures, back in Germany. I knew that for Mongols and Chinese there existed a writing for the blind that would allow me to study these civilizations. That was not the case for Tibet. This led me to conceive — for my own personal use first — braille in Tibetan, which I subsequently wanted to disseminate to all blind people in Tibet.'

'Very good! Excellent!' exclaimed the

visitors. I sensed they were much relieved on learning I had no ulterior political motives. They showed immediate new interest in what I was telling them, asking more details about my projects. I launched into a little exposé in English, as Chungda translated simultaneously. My main goal, I stressed, was that the blind in Tibet be accepted and integrated as full members of society. To this end, my plan was to teach blind children how to read and write, as well as to learn orientation methods. This would enable them with time to go to a 'normal' school, and learn jobs commensurate with their capabilities.

I could hear the visitors talking among themselves, wondering how in the world a blind woman, alone, could possibly tackle this tremendous task satisfactorily. Chungda's translation wasn't faithful: 'The honorable members of the delegation would like to know, what are your personal qualifications?'

'My first job consists in instilling self-confidence in the children, and for that I always start with my own experience. Teaching blind children how to read and write, as well as teaching them how to orient themselves with a cane, is the first step toward bringing them into regular schools. Later they will be taught professions in vocational schools, tailored to their individual capabilities. Thus, with professional skills, they will become equal to other citizens, and their future is assured. They won't depend any longer on charity.'

'But how can a woman who is blind — and alone — carry such a heavy burden?' I overheard them repeat to one another.

'Working with the blind is very exciting to me,' I said. 'With them, I explore the limits of the possible. I always try to raise the bar higher.'

'Absolutely right!' they echoed. 'But who helps you in this noble endeavor?'

'I'm working on assembling a team of motivated and creative teachers. Thanks to the director of the orphanage and his daughter, I have been given the use of this wonderful building. That's a good start. Please look around at what they have made available to me!' Lopsang, clearly satisfied by what I had just told them, interrupted to tell them how, on horseback, I had traveled throughout the country to find blind children in remote villages. I sensed good feelings all around and began to unwind.

How much or how deeply the Chinese delegates really understood and appreciated what I had accomplished will forever remain a mystery to me. Chinese are so polite that real feelings are always hidden behind their strict rules of courtesy. For a European, trying to read how they really feel is virtually impossible.

Two days later it was the turn for European 'experts' — heads of some worldwide humanitarian organization traveling in Central Asia and setting up rehabilitation centers for the visually impaired — to pay me a visit. I was looking forward to what I hoped would be a fruitful exchange, but our dialogue quickly took a diametrically different turn. First I gave them a tour of the school and told them all about our future plans. No reaction. Their silence was increasingly ominous. Then they launched into a systematic denunciation of me personally, and my project. 'You don't have sufficient knowledge or background for all this,' they pronounced. 'It's totally unrealistic. You're not a professional — merely a dilettante, as far as we can judge.'

The inquisition went on. I was accused of jeopardizing the social integrity of the blind by tearing them away from their homes and families, and locking them into a school away from their homes!

'How would you do it differently?' I asked, trying not to show how upset I was. After some hesitation, one of them, I presumed the leader, replied, 'Your endeavor is totally wrong on all counts. Completely erroneous. Integration of the blind must take place in the context of his or her normal environment. Why separate children from their homes? Even if you return them later — education comes *after* integration. You're reversing the process. And that mistake is impossible to rectify!'

I was dumbfounded. 'How in the world can a blind person regain his self-respect — not to mention self-confidence — in a milieu that doesn't trust him? You must not know that in this country a great many blind children live abandoned and forgotten by everybody, including their own parents, existing from hand-to-mouth in dark huts, or worse, forced by their family to beg in the street.'

My two experts remained unmoved by my diatribe. 'You must trust us. We *know*, we have the experience. Real integration can only occur by following our method.'

'You can't have worked in Tibet! I find it difficult to imagine that this method could be used positively here. I would also like to remind you that this territory is three and a half times larger than Germany, with only 2.4 million inhabitants. A great many parts of the country are practically inaccessible. Even the roads, in the winter and during the rainy season, become totally unmanageable. You can't go from one part of the country to the other. Under these conditions, how could anyone take care of and educate blind children in their village of origin?'

Again, no answer.

'As long as blindness is considered a punishment from the gods, as is still often the case here in Tibet, blind people will never become an integral part of any village or society.' I was gaining confidence now. 'Trying to enlighten outsiders won't do it. Only through special education, followed by vocational accomplishments, can the blind integrate properly into Tibetan society. Only as professionals can blind people hope to show they are not inferior to others. But for this to happen, one must give them a proper chance. That's why it is imperative to remove blind children from their usual environment, especially here. They need to learn that there are people out there who *do* trust them. The fundamental priorities lie in educating them, developing their self-confidence, and instilling courage and pride in them. Only after these basic and initial teachings can the blind become part of society.'

I had the feeling that these two experts were less sure of themselves than when they arrived, so I went on. 'When I was very young, my parents discovered I had some eyesight problems. And yet they decided to send me to school like all the other children. This so-called integrated education wasn't ideal, but it was nonetheless very important to me. It enabled me to know the universe of those who can see normally. But all along I felt distinctly different, and I never understood why. Wherever I went, I received privileged treatment. And I noted that some of the teachers addressed themselves to me in a little voice, as if I was helpless, often — just to cite one instance — giving me the biggest portion of cake. I was always asked to enter the classroom first, and be the first to leave. Because of my youth, it didn't occur to me there was anything the matter with my eyes. This said, the frequent cruel jokes played on me made my life a nightmare. One of the favorite jokes was asking me what I thought of someone — a fellow student — who, unbeknownst to me was sitting right next to me, and laughing because I had fallen into their trap. Was there something special about me? And what was it? It took me a while to understand some of the teachers' — and kids' — often nasty attitude toward me. Maybe they were terrified at the idea of becoming blind. Being nasty to me might have been the only way they could confront it, I concluded at the time.

165

'Had I been returned to my cocoon — my family — it would have had the opposite effect: it would have been regression.

'When I turned twelve, I went to a special school for the blind in Marburg. That was a revelation. All of a sudden, for the first time, I discovered I was not alone. It was a great comfort when all the other blind students shared their personal experiences. Teachers as well as students took me seriously for the first time, treating me on equal footing. The friends I quickly made didn't think I was odd. It was the beginning of a new, wonderful life for me.

'I learned to read and write in braille, to navigate comfortably with a white cane. I was sent on errands, and even learned how to cook without help. And what a liberating effect that had on me. Learning how to ski, ride horseback, and row in a kayak, added to the feeling that the world was open to me — providing I used the right techniques to operate.

'My years at the Marburg school for the blind were not only critical, they were a turning point as far as my education was concerned. That school infused in me all the confidence I could possibly have. Without the Marburg teachers' encouragement, I would never have learned and understood the meaning of equal opportunity and equal rights.'

My monologue — probably too long and far too personal — made absolutely no impression on the two gentlemen. Their response made that crystal clear.

'That your scholarly journey was a success, we accept. But don't for one moment think you can apply your own experience to others!' was their only comment.

'As people who can see, I guess you know what's best for those who can't!' I replied, my bitterness showing through.

Once more I was ignored.

'We repeat: it's imperative to establish the right priorities. Focus on integration, not education! And for goodness' sake, don't take children out of their homes!'

Weary beyond description, I blurted out, 'Integration and education are inseparable!'

'In that case,' they concluded, 'we can give you only one piece of advice: take children from Lhasa. That way you'll be able to fulfill both your programs.' And with that they rose to take their leave.

Despite my old self-assurance, these meetings always left me shaken and angry.

16

Everything was in place. At long last the project could begin. But because municipal authorities had so far failed to establish any kind of accurate census of blind people in Tibet, I was at pretty much of a loss to find my future students. All I knew was that there were more of them lost in the anonymity of the cities than out in the countryside, which wasn't much to go on.

But both ophthalmologists and the organization Doctors without Borders helped us locate blind children. And for her part, the always diligent Dolma was relentlessly doing everything in her power to recruit blind children as well, passing the word about our fledgling school as she traveled through the countryside on her medical missions. By June 1998 eight children had been identified. Five had filled out all the necessary forms and were impatient to start school — a modest but encouraging beginning.

It was Dolma who brought us our first charge, a boy named Tendsin. In the course of one of her routine hygiene demonstrations, she had noticed a child in the crowd who appeared distracted and uninterested. She was about to scold him, tell him he must pay attention, when someone whispered to her that the reason he seemed so absent was simply that he couldn't see.

'You're blind?' she asked the young boy.

'Of course,' Tendsin replied matter-of-factly.

Dolma wasted no time making her usual pitch for the school, explaining to the boy what our teaching could mean for his future. His reaction was immediate: he started stamping his foot impatiently.

'So when can I start? What do I have to do to get in?'

'If you follow my instructions — and that means washing yourself well morning and night — Kelsang Meto will come in a car, and bring you to the school in Lhasa. I'll want to talk to your parents,' Dolma said. 'We'll need their permission.'

'I'm sure they'll give it,' he said. 'Come, I'll take you to my mother.'

Again explaining the point and purpose of the school, Dolma saw quickly that the mother needed no convincing.

'Promise you won't be long,' Tendsin said.

'I promise,' Dolma answered him, delighted by his enthusiasm.

The promise was soon kept. Within days,

Lopsang's jeep drove us to Tendsin's village, with Chungda in tow as an interpreter.

It was a rather big village. A *mola* — grandmother — volunteered to lead us to the blind boy's house.

Tendsin's six-year-old brother was standing in front of the entrance of a rather simple hut. Alerted by the little boy's shouts, his mother materialized, welcoming us warmly. 'Ever since Tendsin first heard about the school,' she told us, 'he has been scrubbing his face and hands every morning and evening. But when no one came to fetch him, he became depressed, afraid no one ever would. Tendsin is out at the moment. He just took the animals to the fields. Do please come in.'

She sent the little screamer to go get his brother, offered us some *tchang*, sat down beside us, and, as is often the case in Tibet, unburdened herself as we sat listening quietly to her tale of woes. Abandoned early on by her husband, she had brought the two boys up alone, which was a terrible hardship.

'Tendsin's becoming difficult to control,' she lamented, 'but I am thankful he can spend his energies out in the fields with the animals.'

As for her younger one, he seemed afraid of his own shadow, tied to her apron string. 'He isn't even blind, and he behaves like a handicapped child!' she added.

Half an hour later, Tendsin arrived, out of breath from running. Nine years old, he seemed extremely alert for his age.

'I've been waiting to meet you for so long!' was his cheerful greeting. Turning toward his mother, he asked, 'Can I go right now with them to Lhasa?'

It took but a few minutes for him to gather his meager belongings into a neat little bundle. After dashing out to say good-bye to his friends and relatives, he soon returned, announcing that he was more than ready.

At least some things happen faster here than anywhere else in the world! I thought. A pity those uptight European authorities couldn't have witnessed this scene! 'The one thing you can't do is tear children away from their families!' was still ringing in my ears. Here in Tibet, however, no one ever mistook us for child robbers. Generally the entire village came out to wish us good luck.

I had invited — as I always did — Tendsin's mother to come with us and stay for a few days, until her son adjusted to his new life. But that evening, she announced she had decided not to come along to Lhasa. She was confident Tendsin would adapt quickly and easily. Her real concerns were for her six-year-old whom she would have to turn over to his grandmother while she was away. And the *mola* was prone to worry and fret about her younger grandchild. No, it was too difficult to leave her younger son behind.

As for most of the other blind pupils' parents I met, not only would it not have occurred to any of them to think negatively about sending their child to our school, but time and again, I had the distinct impression that the families were actually relieved at the prospect of not having to care for their 'good-for-nothing' child anymore.

Take twelve-year-old Tashi, for example. He had been located for us by the governor of a distant district. Tashi's was a backward village, with no electricity. No car or truck had ever been seen there. We arrived at the village in our jeep and were surprised that the only people gathered to meet us were *molas* and *polas* — all toothless. Did the entire population of this place consist of elderly people? we wondered. The younger ones, including Tashi's parents, we were told, were out working in the fields, along with the yaks and goats.

'Where's the blind boy?' asked Chungda.

'Locked up in his house, so nothing bad can happen to him,' the *molas* explained.

Tashi's mother soon arrived and, as she led us to her house, begged Chungda to please,

please take her son back with us. When Chungda first saw Tashi, he appeared listless, bereft, abandoned. The only person Tashi seemed to communicate with, we were told, was his father.

'What about Tashi's father?' I asked. 'Where is he?'

We decided to wait for him, and we did, for hours and hours. But it was worth the wait. When finally he did show up, Tashi came immediately to life. We watched as the two engaged in a long, animated exchange. Very excited, Tashi was filling his father's ears about the school. Witnessing this bond, and the energy that suddenly flowed in the boy, we pleaded with the father to accompany his son back to Lhasa. Much to our surprise, he accepted.

As we were ready to leave, one of the villagers stopped us: 'Can you stay on here a bit longer?' she said. 'There's a nine-year-old blind girl possessed by the devil in the next village. Could you go see her?'

Intrigued, we set off for her village. In contrast to Tendsin's, this village seemed modern, even quite prosperous, boasting a number of big houses, all with electricity. This surprising prosperity was the direct result of a warm spring nearby that had for centuries been considered holy and attracted pilgrims from around the world. An impressive medical facility and a spa had also been built there.

We were received by the girl's grandmother. The child who had been described to us as a nine-year-old turned out to be a sweet little three-year-old, whose answers to our questions were simple and direct. We offered her some fruit, which she accepted, thanking us profusely.

While the little girl was sitting on the floor, playing with the fruit, her grandmother told us she would be more than happy to be relieved of her obligations vis-à-vis the child. Her older sister, she explained, who had had perfect eyesight, had recently died after a long illness, and the family was not up to coping with the three-year-old.

'I would have preferred that this one go rather than her sister!' her grandmother hissed. 'What's more, there's no doubt this child is possessed by the devil!' Coming closer to us, she whispered, 'She's dangerous, you know She can see *everything*. She gets around as if she had both her eyes. I'm sure she can even see our *thoughts!*'

How in the world could any grandmother speak of her own granddaughter this way? I wondered. Sadly, we couldn't be of help to her: she was too young to come to our school.

It demoralized me to think we had to leave her behind.

Not long thereafter, Doctors without Borders told us about a blind boy by the name of Norbu. His parents had learned about our school and were impatiently hoping for a visit. Wasting no time, we sought out the tiny village, which consisted of no more than ten houses lined up along a narrow hill path. Goats, chickens, dogs, and children were everywhere underfoot. Even inside Norbu's house, chickens were flying hither and yon, making a terrible racket; a lamb and some baby goats were lying on beds of straw, while a piglet was noisily voicing its forceful opinion. Then, in the midst of all this madness, in flew a small boy, nearly the size of a dwarf, who in a high-pitched voice, announced, 'I'm Norbu, and I'm nine years old!'

He apparently looked more like a four-year-old, and Chungda adamantly refused to believe the boy was in fact nine.

In Tibet, getting accurate data — for example, a child's real age — is virtually impossible. Because birth records do not exist, parents themselves often get confused. One has to remember that in this country, traditionally a baby is one year old the day he or she is born. A baby born just before the

Tibetan New Year is two years old within a few days!

'You came to take Norbu away, didn't you? Exactly what will he be doing in your school, anyway?' His grand-parents seemed worried.

'He will learn to read and write!' Chungda responded.

Norbu's parents echoed Chungda and added, 'In any case, he'll never have the opportunity to learn anything in this village.'

The grandfather, voicing his concern about 'losing' his grandchild in a louder and louder voice, had managed to frighten the chickens, which had retreated to a corner, while Norbu began crying silently.

Heavy of heart, I remembered my two European experts' visit. Had they been present, it would have corroborated everything they had warned me and admonished me about. Their leitmotiv, 'Make sure never to take children from their families!' was echoing in my mind.

It was clear: if the grandfather's word was final, Norbu would not be allowed to come with us.

Doing my best to console the sobbing boy, I suggested his father come along with Norbu to make sure that all went well. That seemed to reassure them, and finally the grandparents relented.

In addition to Tendsin, Tashi, and Norbu, we also had among our first official pupils Chila and Kunchong — two little balls of raw energy I had spotted a year before, in the Drigung district.

As far as we could judge, Chila was eight. His reputation of being the storyteller in his village preceded him. At the slightest provocation, he broke into songs, most of which he had made up. Since he was very little, he would go sit on a stone in the middle of the village square, regaling the other children with his stories. As the permanent entertainer, no one ever gave him any responsible tasks to perform. As a result, the little entertainer had become lazy, lost in his dreams. Later, at our school in Lhasa, we often caught him sitting in the shadow of a pear tree, performing for his schoolmates, even talking to stray animals that were passing by. As soon as a teacher approached, Chila would clap his hands in the air, chase him away, and in a strident voice break into one of his songs.

I decided to take Kunchog, another energetic younger fellow — who was probably five or six — immediately in hand. When we arrived at his village, he couldn't wait to lead us to the fountain and show to us how well he had learned to wash himself — and not only his hands and face but his clothes as well. When I offered to take him to Lhasa for a trial period at our school, his father responded enthusiastically.

Our school now had five registered pupils — all boys. Meto was our first girl. Holding her mother's hand, she arrived at the school in the middle of the night. I had already fallen asleep when the doorman woke me. Worried that one of our boys was sick or homesick, I slipped into my clothes and headed straight to the dormitory. Passing through the kitchen, I found Palden and Anila sitting at the kitchen table with the little girl and her parents, drinking salted butter tea. Upon hearing about our school from an ophthalmologist, they had immediately packed Meto's things and without further ado come directly to Lhasa. Never mind that it was the middle of the night!

When we asked the shy, clearly frightened little girl questions, she would bury her face in her hands, stare downward, and mutter some unintelligible monosyllabic answers.

'How old are you?' we asked.

'Twelve,' she whispered, trying to hide behind her mother.

She still had a bit of sight, her parents told us. When Meto was eight, she and some friends came upon an old grenade. The grenade exploded. One of her friends lost a hand, another's leg had to be amputated. Meto was the most seriously wounded. She lost both her eyes. After four operations, she could barely see enough to find her way around.

'Did she go back to school after the accident?' I asked.

'Oh, no!' sighed her mother. 'None of the teachers welcomed her back. Ever since the accident she's been staying home, helping me clean the house. That's all.'

The family lived in a suburb of Lhasa. Since her accident, Meto had never gone outside the house and never seen her classmates again. In fact, her mother strictly forbade her to play outside, for fear of another accident.

Anila leaned down to Meto and asked, 'How would you like to come to this school, and learn with other blind children?'

'I would,' whispered Meto with as much enthusiasm as her fearful state could summon.

Meto stayed with us as a boarding student. While her mother could easily have brought her each morning and picked her up in the afternoon, that she stay as a boarder seemed preferable to all of us — at least in the beginning. She needed a cocoon, a protected zone where she could build up her self-confidence and no longer be afraid of others.

17

Anything but becoming a teacher! I remember swearing to myself when I was little. And here I was on this lovely morning, about to teach my first class! The sun still wasn't up when I awoke. It was early for Tibetans. From a larger perspective, one should take one's time to face such a new day.

Crossing the courtyard with my pail to fetch my morning water at the well, I heard some sweet children's voices like that of a choir chanting morning prayers. It wasn't the orphans: their side of the school was totally silent. I put down my pail and walked over to our school. From the classroom, I recognized Meto's raspy voice.

'Your turn, Norbu!'

Could this be the same shy Meto I had so recently seen? The scared little girl had metamorphosed herself into an authoritarian celebrant. Little Norbu, with his high-pitched voice, was dutifully repeating verses Meto was feeding him. When Kunchog became distracted, or Chila broke into one of his singing creations, she would bang on the table with a ruler, and as soon as order had returned,

Lake Namtso, the highest saltwater lake in the world, which Sabriye 'saw' and described vividly.

Sabriye and Paul when they first met in the Banak Shol hotel in 1997.

Anila, who has been with the project from the beginning, is like a mother to the children.

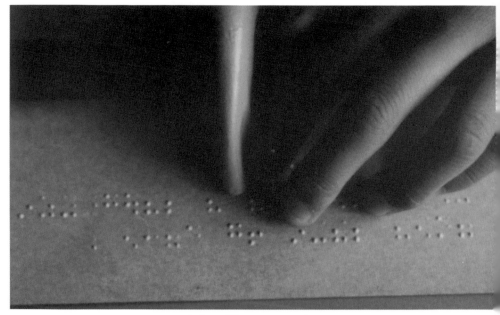

A braille typewriter.

Sabriye teaching Chila the basics of braille.

Sonam Bongso teaching braille to Kjumi with the help of Velcro dots. Sabriye and Paul developed this system to train the children's motor skills before they learn formal braille, which uses smaller dots.

Sabriye with Yudon.

Sabriye teaching Yudon, Tendsin, and Nyima how to use their canes in front of the Potala, the Dalai Lama's winter palace in Lhasa.

Gyendsen playing soccer. The ball contains a small bell that enables him to locate it in space.

Tendsin high on his horse.

*Kjumi enjoying a
painting class.*

*Sonam Bongso doing
her hair.*

Sabriye with Kjumi and Nordon.

ABOVE: *The rooftop classroom in our newly built school. Nordon's mother sold us her house, making it possible for us to build proper accommodations for a comfortable living and teaching environment.*
BELOW: *Tendsin taking a braille test on the rooftop.*

Sangpo, one of the blind teachers, conducting a class in the new building.

The children performing **Drowa Sangmo,** *a Tibetan play.*

A Buddhist nun who lives in a cave 12,800 feet above the Lhasa Valley.

Prayer flags on a Himalayan pass, 17,700 feet above sea level.

made them all pray together in a loud voice. Such a rapid and rewarding transformation warmed my heart.

A strong smell of salted butter wafted from the nearby kitchen, where Anila was already preparing tea. The idea of drinking tea with butter this early in the morning was more than I could envisage. I tiptoed away.

Class was to start at nine. Teaching the basic principles of writing for the blind was the order of the day. I was apprehensive, because I had to face the class alone. Palden, on whom I had counted for support, still owed some teaching time to the orphanage.

Without any schooling in child psychology, nor any teacher training or experience, how in the world could I possibly pull off what I was facing? I was nervous, but also painfully aware that all these children were of different ages, characters, backgrounds; what was more, I would be teaching in a language I knew only imperfectly.

In order to learn braille, one needs to know how to count to six, at least. Each braille character has from one to six little points in relief. The left point represents the digit 1, the point underneath is number 2, and the last of the row is 3; the right-hand point is 4. Meto and I rolled dough — tsampas — into tiny little balls or marbles with our hands. I handed each child two bowls, one empty, the other with six little *tsampa* dough marbles. The exercise quickly turned into a game of passing the *tsampa* balls from one bowl to the other while counting out loud: 'Dchig, ni, sum, nga, drug!' The children, I was happy to see, seemed to be thoroughly enjoying the exercise. Assuming, however, that all this was but a prelude to my teaching them a song, they showed disappointment and resisted learning how to count. Counting was not what they had in mind.

I needed to come up with another trick. After some quick strategizing, I lined them up in a row and started counting them one by one, attaching a name to a number: 'Tashi, *dchig*, Norbu, *ni*, Meto, *drug*,' and so on. Then I placed myself in the row, and each child in turn counted us. It worked. They understood. They became so carried away and excited that they started counting everything around them — table, chairs, windows, fingers. Tashi however, convinced this was a singing class, kept on singing, 'Dchig, ni, sum . . . ,' at the top of his lungs.

At noon, I announced that class was over. Our meal, prepared in the orphanage's central kitchen, was carried to our dining hall by Anila in a large pot. She was dishing out generous portions of rice and boiled cabbage

— a balanced if not particularly appetizing meal. The children wolfed it down in no time flat.

Now it was time for their nap. They all marched off to their dormitory while I repaired to my room, where I was looking forward to refueling after the morning's emotions. I had barely sat down when I heard a few knocks on the door. 'Kelsang Meto!?' It was Anila, who sounded in a state of panic. She took my arm and led me to the school.

'What's happening?'

'Tschu! Tschu!' (Water, water!) was all she said.

We hurried across the courtyard, and as we approached the school, I understood. Both the floor and walls were completely drenched, and screams of joy could be heard everywhere.

On their way to their nap, the children had discovered the shower. In a state of great excitement, they turned it on full blast, refusing to let go of this new toy, with its endless possibilities. Water pouring out of the wall! What fun! They had never encountered anything like it and were screaming, out of control. Jumping up and down, naked as the day they were born, they chased any intruder who chanced upon them, hosing him mercilessly with cold water.

Norbu, Kunchog, and Tendsin were the most excited. All three had filled their shoes with water and run to the balcony, and were joyfully pouring the contents onto anyone who happened to walk beneath. I was drenched from head to toe, at the mercy of these demented children. As for Meto, Tashi, and Chila, they had gone to the terrace to dry their clothes, and were giggling loudly at each stage of 'Operation Water.' Drenched like the rest of us, Palden had a sudden inspiration. All one needed to do to stop this folly, he shouted, was turn off the shower faucet. No sooner said than done. The flood mercifully stopped.

We were facing another problem now: we had not yet provided for any change of clothes for the children, which meant that after hanging up their clothes to dry on the balcony, we had no choice but to send all of them back to bed.

Later that afternoon, when they were back in their dry garments, class resumed. This time Palden was there to assist me. Braille was being taught to the older ones, and my lack of fluent Tibetan would have made the job hard. In Lopsang's studio I had created little slate blackboards with sticky Velcro rectangles, which were given to each child, along with six felt circles that could be removed at will.

Numbers were announced slowly by Palden, indicating the points' position in the braille alphabet. The pupils would then place their felt circles on the corresponding positions. For Meto, Tendsin, and Norbu, who had quickly understood the principle, it was child's play. Tashi much preferred putting the felt pieces in his mouth and chewing them well, while Kunchog ran uncontrollably up and down the classroom, flailing his little blackboard on his classmates' heads. As for Chila, he was repeating his instructions and, having memorized them quickly, turning them into joyful songs.

Despite this chaos, the day had nonetheless been a kind of success, I thought: a teaching session had turned into an enormous entertainment. The floor was strewn with *tsampa* balls and felt circles. Kunchog's blackboard ended up broken into a thousand pieces on the floor as well. And to crown it all — probably because of the excitement of the school's first day, and because his father had gone back home — Chila had peed in his pants!

I was surprised that neither Norbu nor Kunchog had cried after the other fathers had returned home that morning. Norbu, happy to have found a friend in Tendsin, encouraged his father to leave in peace. As for Kunchog, he was no doubt too little to have realized that his father had left. All in all, to my surprise, all five appeared to have quickly adjusted to their radical change of life. The only one heartbroken by his father's departure was Tashi, who was sobbing uncontrollably on his bed, refusing to play with any of his new comrades.

After class I escaped to my little garden, hoping to catch a few moments of peace and sun. My moment of calm was short-lived. 'Kelsang Meto! Kelsang Meto! Hurry, follow me!' It was Palden, knocking at the front door of my garden.

A group of adults and children were assembled in the courtyard, along with the orphanage kids. As soon as they saw me, they yelled in chorus:

'Kunchog! Kunchog! He has disappeared!'

Everyone had looked high and low for him, but he was nowhere to be found.

Kunchog had undoubtedly run out to look for his father, or had simply decided to go home, I concluded. I was terribly concerned: after all, he was only six years old, and my responsibility. Should I tell the police? If I didn't and we didn't find him, what should I do?

As I was mulling all this, I felt someone

tugging on my sleeve; it was Tendsin, whispering something in my ear. There was so much noise around, I had to ask him to repeat it several times. 'I know where Kunchog is,' he said. Taking me by the hand, he led me to the gate, out into an alleyway, and over to the teaching building. Of all our blind children, Tendsin was the best integrated in his village of origin. Back home, while the village children were at school, the head of the village had entrusted Tendsin with keeping an eye on his yaks and goats of the neighbors. He was always able to tell the animals apart by the sound of their bells. Very sharp and alert, he learned to read and write in Tibetan braille in a mere few weeks, and assimilated the basics of English and Chinese in braille in only two months. In no time at all, he could follow the regular primary school program. Despite all these qualities, there was nothing arrogant or pushy about him. He was everyone's friend, always ready to give a helping hand, whether it meant accompanying Tashi to the toilet, pocketing extra cakes with Norbu from the orphanage kitchen, or joining the house mother in making beds, cleaning, or washing the dishes.

Here again he was showing a degree of maturity by not yielding to the general hysteria. I noticed that Palden and Anila were following us, along with the orphanage kids. We must have been an interesting sight — a little shepherd leading three adults and a gang of excited little rascals. Tendsin was marching before his troop with remarkable assurance. I knew few blind, even with a sense of orientation, who would have been as poised, as capable, as he was. I was about to ask him where we were going when I heard the orphanage kids shout, 'Here he is!'

And there was Kunchog, making his way down the road, in excellent spirits, totally unaware he might have done anything wrong. We found him following the side of the road, heading toward the center of Lhasa, hopping and singing and brandishing two or three little bills his father had given him as pocket money. Lost? Not at all, he told us, all he was doing was going to town to buy some toys for himself and his friends! After thanking him for his good intentions, we steered him, more than a trifle disappointed, back to the house. When calm returned and the children were fed and sent off to bed that evening, I retired to my office. A letter to my German sponsoring organization was in order. I was worried they had abandoned me. Since my return to Lhasa I had not heard a word from them, even though I had written a number of letters pleading for the money due me. The sums they were supposed to be transferring to my Tibetan account so that I could repay Lopsang and Chungda for all the school furniture and materials they had kindly bought had never arrived. This I found extremely upsetting. The fact was, they had put me in a desperate situation. I needed money to pay salaries, and buy food and clothes for the children. Our school was living off credit, but time was up. Trying to overcome my irritation and the sense of urgency, I forced myself to write a friendly letter. Several weeks went by, and that letter, like the preceding ones, also remained unanswered.

I didn't know what to do next, having already nearly exhausted my personal income.

18

One fine June night it began to rain, and it rained night and day without stop until the end of August. During that summer of 1998, natural catastrophes followed one after the other. In many places on the Tibetan plateau, those torrential rains made mountains literally melt away, taking with them whole villages and fields. Houses disappeared. Tremendous casualties were reported. Bridges were destroyed by enormous masses of water; the carcasses of trucks were seen floating in swollen rivers; and from one end of the country to the other, buses were crushed by stone avalanches and mudslides. Tibetans were apparently accustomed to such catastrophes, it was part and parcel of their lives, but for me it took on dramatic proportions.

While Western meteorologists were losing themselves in conjectures about the abnormal behavior of El Niño and the warm current of the Pacific, Tibetans turned to metaphysical explanations. Rumor had it that in a village near Gyantse, a child was born covered with little eyes — a sure sign it was a terrible demon! The codirector of the Red Cross, a

Tibetan, had publicly confirmed that this child had to be the cause of all the cataclysms. Many of my Tibetan friends, convinced of the demon's existence, had covered themselves with protective amulets.

It always surprised and amused me to see that here in Tibet ancient ancestral superstitions and the modern world of technology operated in tandem. A Tibetan CEO I had met — modern, quite sophisticated, wearing a black leather jacket, using a cell phone, and driving the latest model jeep — was totally transformed one day. What had happened to so change him? One of his employees was killed in one of the company's jeeps, he told me. As his boss, he, the CEO, bore full responsibility for the employee's death and deeply believed, in keeping with local legend, that the man's spirit would come back to cause the death of three more people. Mutual friends told me the CEO kept in constant communication with that spirit. I found it difficult to reconcile such contradictory beliefs. A Dutch woman who worked in a development organization happened to visit him one day and found him about to slit his throat. She quickly intervened, and in the nick of time prevented what would have been the man's tragic death. The mysteries, ambiguities, and contradictions of the Tibetan culture will never cease to fascinate me.

In addition to the relentless rain, in Tibet it was unusually cold for the season. Above 18,000 feet high, the world was blanketed with snow. Both the persistent rain and the unusual cold became the subject of endless theories. One Red Cross colleague of Paul in Shigatse, modern in his views of the world, offered Paul the following explanation for the strange climatic shift: 'There are more and more solar ovens in Tibet — consisting of two aluminum reflectors concentrating the sun's rays onto a large recipient — which are used to boil water. These solar ovens absorb the sun's energy, don't you see,' she said, dead serious, 'and have already lowered the sun's level in the sky by eighteen inches in the course of a year — thus the change in temperature!'

When Paul, amused, passed this story on to Dolma, she answered, 'Not true! Tibetans aren't the only ones responsible! The Chinese also have solar ovens, so they're partly responsible!'

Whatever the reason, I had never experienced such persistent and torrential rain, an interminable deluge, worthy of Noah himself. I prayed that the walls of our school, built only a year ago, would prove sound. But I was asking too much. Puddles of water soon began appearing both in the bedrooms and in my office. Unfazed by it all, Lopsang wasn't at all interested in having the roof repaired. Chungda, to whom I had brought my problem, responded by saying that no repairs could be made until I repaid all I owed them. I was extremely embarrassed; I had no response to that. Another pleading letter to my sponsoring organization was in order, and I promised Chungda I would write them that day. She agreed that the roof situation needed to be addressed, but said there was nothing they could do until my money arrived. I felt terrible at my complete inability to remedy this predicament.

As the hours and days passed, larger and larger puddles appeared everywhere. With the help of Anila and Palden, we stretched sheets of plastic, creating a kind of awning that gave us some vague protection, but this was no solution.

I told Chungda that if her father continued to refuse repair for the roof, his buildings would literally dissolve, and he would lose the value of his investments.

'We still haven't received any money transfer from you in our account!' she tossed back at me. 'I trust you understood me! As long as we haven't received your money, we have no intention of lifting a finger for you or your school!'

'But how can I let children sleep in those puddles?' I asked full of sadness. 'It isn't *their* fault my German organization hasn't kept its commitment and sent me my money!'

Without deigning to reply, Chungda turned and walked away, leaving me standing there in the rain. I remained there statuelike, water dripping down my back, and began to shiver uncontrollably. Resigned, and with a sense of defeat, I returned to my office. No one, it had become clear, cared anymore in the least about my school; from now on I would have to bear every responsibility — the children, the teachers, and the daily upkeep — as well as finding a new source of funding. My only hope was that Lopsang would understand my predicament, show a forgiving heart, and relent about the roof repair. But that was not to be.

Not long thereafter, on one of the rare sunny days since the rainy season had begun, an unfortunate incident occurred that did little to endear me or us to Lopsang and his daughter.

That morning, the children had been exceptionally attentive in class. Even Kunchog, who usually enjoyed running away with the little slate blackboards of his friends, which he would smash, had been good. He was sitting next to a tried Tashi, who was softly singing him a song. Norbu, Tendsin, and Meto, who from their fourth day of class had mastered the first twelve braille characters in Tibetan, were busy helping Chila recognize letters and numbers by guiding his fingers over the reliefs of the characters on his blackboard.

To reward them for their good work, I had organized a ball game. Both Palden and Anila had trouble understanding how blind people could actually play ball! Simple. Here's how: I had inserted rice inside water-polo balloons. As the ball moved, the rice would shake inside, and the kids, instead of seeing the ball come to them as seeing children do, would hear it, and be able to determine its position. It worked very well for all of us. All would have been fine except for the lawn behind the school, which was soaking wet from all the rain, definitely not the ideal field for a ball game. But despite the puddles and mud, everyone was having a good time. In fact, the messy playing field probably doubled their fun. The ball game soon turned into a game of mud throwing. They all roared with laughter when Kunchog managed to shove a fistful of mud down Tendsin's shirt. Even little Tashi, who was holding on to Palden's hand for dear life, was trying to dodge the bombardment of mud around him. As for Norbu, who was the most agile of the players but also the most out of control, as soon as he caught the ball he would run as fast as his short legs permitted, jumping over puddles and piles of mud. He would also — whenever he felt it strategically useful — stand still until the rice rattling inside the ball stopped, so not to betray his position. But Meto, blessed as she was with her tiny bit of remaining eyesight, always managed to find him as he was trying to control his giggles. All in all, they were all having such a happy time that we let them play and enjoy until a dark cloud covered the sun and it started to rain again. The temperature quickly dropped, and in a matter of minutes everyone began to shiver, including me.

After that wonderful afternoon of mud-slinging, we had of course planned to put the children under the shower and dress them in fresh clothes.

While Palden was getting the showers ready, I asked Anila to fetch some dry clothes. But she did not respond, acting dumb. Hadn't she heard me? I repeated. With great reluctance she confessed that there were no other clothes. It was now my turn to think I hadn't heard properly. Palden confirmed what Anila had said. I was flabbergasted. Hadn't Chungda assured me some time back that she had gone to town to buy fresh clothes? She had even described the clothes in detail to me: 'They were so cute, so becoming!'

Not a word was true. I was speechless. Day after day, the children had gone to class wearing the same miserable rags. And all this time I had no idea that Chungda had reneged! Why had Palden and Anila never told me?

Having no choice, we decided to wash the clothes by hand and put the children to bed while waiting for the clean clothes to dry. With my own pittance of personal money I had held in reserve, I sent Anila to town to buy what she could in the way of new clothes.

Upset, I marched off to Chungda. A serious talk was in order: that, it turned out, was a grave mistake. While she admitted she had lied, the consequences of that heated confrontation quickly turned my life into sheer living hell.

Chungda went on the warpath. She did everything she could think of every day to block my efforts and sabotage my work. Life had become increasingly difficult. They would regularly pull Palden out of class and send him on some ridiculous errand. These interruptions and absences in our teaching program were harmful to both me and the children. I complained, to no avail. Palden owed them his time, she reminded me. But in what I took to be a gesture of goodwill or reconciliation, Chungda offered to substitute for Palden. Wanting to keep a modicum of good relations with her and her father, I accepted. I should have known better. Chungda never kept her word. She was always otherwise engaged when it came time to meet me in class, and I was inevitably left in the lurch, to do the teaching alone.

Meanwhile, as days and weeks went by, I still had no word from Germany or my sponsors! I was beginning to despair. Could I continue to carry alone all the responsibilities of the school? With no immediate solution in sight, I felt hopelessly trapped.

★ ★ ★

As Tendsin and Norbu were drying puddles in their room one happy day, Paul appeared at my door. His first mission for the Red Cross at the other end of Tibet was finished, and he was back in Lhasa for good.

'What's going on, here? Is there a problem?' I briefed him as best I could about all that had happened.

Grabbing a ladder from the orphanage, he climbed onto the roof and wasted no time patching it up, concentrating on the non-waterproofed spots. Lopsang was greatly impressed.

He had every reason to be grateful, for without Paul's timely intervention, his sumptuous new buildings would have suffered serious damage from the endless rains. He momentarily overcame any bitterness he held against me and, to my surprise, invited us both to dinner. I was tense at first, remembering all of our hosts' misdeeds, but soon everyone settled into a good mood and relaxed.

'Your buildings are beautiful,' said Paul, in an outburst of combined truth and diplomacy. 'But there are some minor construction issues that should be addressed before anything else happens to the building's overall solidity.'

Lopsang sighed. He was aware that the construction wasn't perfect, he admitted, but not being an architect, he had been unable to tell exactly what needed to be done.

Paul offered to help. He wanted no salary. 'Just a roof over his head, and some food.'

'We'd be delighted to accept your offer, and welcome you to stay in one of our guest rooms. That way, you'll also be able to help Kelsang Meto.'

I was very pleased by this new turn of events. Paul proved useful to everyone. And everyone liked him, from the orphanage employees to the children. Chungda had just bought a computer and knew very little about how it worked. Paul showed her how. He also lent a hand in keeping the book of accounts for our school.

It looked as if, with some luck, we would be able to pay our debts in the near future and eliminate all the problems I'd been having with Chungda and her father. My parents were due in Lhasa shortly. I had asked them to take some money out of my savings and bring it with them, hoping that would fill the gap until my sponsoring organization hopefully gave some sign of life.

19

Tibet seems to attract a particular kind of Western tourist who, after the initial discovery and exploration of the country, decides to stay on, looking desperately for something 'meaningful' to do.

Dora was such a person. She had landed on my doorstep a few days after Paul's return, as we were in the throes of some momentary school chaos. I was in the middle of briefing Chungda about the ways we operated — she had expressed the desire to get more involved in the school. For some unknown reason, Chila was sobbing, and we were trying to deal with his problems while at the same time Norbu was racing back and forth making loud noises as if he were a truck. As for Tendsin and Meto, they were having a nice little fight, banging each other over the head with their blackboards. Earlier that day, Kunchog's father had come by the school to fetch his son. The boy had proved too young, too immature, to be away from home, and too young for our program. As they left, we made sure to tell father and son that Kunchog would always be welcome, and encouraged them to try us later when Kunchog felt ready to leave home. This loss, however, had undoubtedly unsettled our tight little group of children, which explained their unprecedented out-of-control behavior of the last two hours.

Standing on the threshold of our entrance and visibly shocked by what she was witnessing, Dora nonetheless managed to introduce herself and, without hesitation or being invited, stepped inside. She was German and had worked previously as a social worker. She also held a degree in art therapy and specialized pedagogy. Surely, she thought, with all her qualifications, we would offer her a job on the spot!

As tactfully as I could, I gently suggested she come back some other time. As she could see, this was an ill-chosen moment for interviewing her, or anyone, for that matter. I hoped this would send her away.

But apparently she wasn't the type to take no for an answer. 'Is there anyone who can actually see here?' she peremptorily asked.

'Why such a question! This is a school for the blind,' I replied.

'But you do need someone with eyesight to help supervise your various activities, don't you?'

I turned, pointing to Chungda, and said,

'As you can see, I'm in the process of training that very person.'

Ignoring my reply, Dora bent down and sat next to Chila, who immediately proceeded to hide under the table and yell at the top of his lungs. Momentarily defeated, she tried her luck elsewhere and walked over to Tashi, who was sitting in a corner, tearing a paper napkin to shreds. She sat down quietly next to him and began talking to him in the sugary, reassuring voice adopted by all 'specialized pedagogues,' ostensibly continuing to ignore me.

The bell rang. It was noon. Relieved that the difficult morning had at last come to an end, I went to seek a little peace and quiet in my little apartment. I had just put water to heat in the kettle for some tea when I heard a knock at the door. It was Dora.

'I apologize if I am disturbing you. But from what I could observe, I assure you that you *do* need the help of a qualified teacher.'

'I have Palden, an experienced teacher who does a wonderful job, and besides, conventional recipes don't interest me. I'm better off doing it my own way.'

'Well, in any case, you could use a good organizer. Someone competent, who holds the right degrees.'

I held my breath, trying to find something to say in reply.

'All I can say, once again, is that judging from what I saw this morning, you clearly don't seem capable of staying on top of things. Obviously not by yourself!'

'I never intended to handle things by myself. I'm in the process of recruiting Tibetan collaborators, who will help me develop a structure as well as teaching methods that correspond to local conditions.'

'Tibetans haven't a clue about pedagogy!' she spat out.

'They seem to be doing a fine job of raising their kids. And anyway, I don't believe in imposing our Western methods on Tibetans.'

There followed a long and heated monologue in which Dora, I'm sorry to say, became the target of all my pent-up anger against those bureaucrats and so-called professionals who had patronized me with the attitude; 'Oh, this poor naive little blind girl who doesn't know anything. We really must show her how it's properly done!'

'You're not equipped for learning this difficult language!' my German professor had warned me years before, when I told him I wanted to study Tibetan.

'Better get that idea out of your head right away. It's simply not realistic!' said another,

204

upon hearing I wanted to travel alone to Tibet.

'You'll never make it!' a big shot from one of those humanitarian organizations had told me when I presented my school project. How many roadblocks had I stumbled over on my way to Tibet!

I'd had enough! I felt nothing but disdain for those officials who were incapable of ridding themselves of their long-encrusted, preestablished ideas. Bureaucrats who operate like robots, reciting rules from a book, unable to view without prejudice any project that seems out of the ordinary, are decidedly not for me.

'No, I'm sorry, Dora, but there's no job here for someone like you!' I finished.

My tirade had welled up from some unknown depth in my soul. I realized I had given the poor woman more than she had bargained for. But it did the job; she left to pursue other adventures elsewhere.

Not long thereafter, one day while Paul had gone to the market to buy some fruit, vegetables, and pancakes for breakfast, I was in the middle of writing one of my endless fund-raising letters when someone I had briefly met the year before entered my office, uninvited and unexpected. He tapped his fingers on my desk to attract my attention.

'My name is Kurt,' he began. 'We met briefly a year ago. And you're the famous Sabriye! I've heard a great deal about you!' All this in the silly, irritating voice some adults feel compelled to use when speaking to babies or the very young.

'I think you're marvelous, too!' I replied, echoing his sugary tone. It did the trick. He registered his mistake and pursued in a normal voice. 'As you might remember, I am a psychotherapist. I'm writing a book on the subconscious, and I hope to be able to hide somewhere away from it all, in some spiritual place like a cave, to pursue my research. While I'm waiting for the Tibetan authorities to grant me permission to go live in a cave, I'm staying at the Banak Shol.'

Kurt's intrusion into my morning work annoyed me more than I can say. I decided to finish my letter and let him wait. I bent back to my writing, to no avail. He tapped me on the shoulder: 'You could at least give me a few minutes of your time! By the way, it might be important to you!'

'Would you like to make yourself useful? Go across the field where Anila and the children are. She's breaking her back trying to work the land after the rain. She is hoping to create a vegetable garden for the school.'

'Me? Useful? Of course, I'd be delighted.

You have no reason to know, but the book I am writing is going to be sensational — a best-seller, I'm sure.'

'Great! But what does that have to do with our school?'

'The book will bring in a lot of money. I'm ready to forgo twenty-five percent of the profit and donate it to the school, in exchange for a job and a room here. The State Department told me that if I presented a signed employment contract, that would expedite my other affairs. Could you hire me? Of course, that would entail a room for me here — '

'Wait a minute. Slow down. I can't just hire anyone who walks in here. Nor can I give you a room just like that. I have no control of the rooms here.'

Another tap on my shoulder.

'I'm not just anyone! We've known each other for at least a year!'

I was dumbfounded. This guy couldn't tell the difference between meeting someone a year ago and knowing that person for a year. Some psychotherapist! Besides, I was in no mood for his kind of familiarity or pushiness.

'To tell you the truth, I find it problematic every time I hear of westerners wanting to establish permanent residency in Tibet. Starting with myself. I have daily scruples, even though in my case, I only plan to remain here for three or four years at the most.'

'You shouldn't judge people like me so harshly,' he said in his best psychotherapeutic tone. 'All we want to do is help others. As for myself, I have a real Saint Bernard syndrome!'

That made me explode.

'That wonderful syndrome reminds me of those people back home who, without asking, take my arm and cross me to the other side of the street. That's precisely the same patronizing way most westerners act in Tibet. We land here from a totally different culture and immediately assume we should tell Tibetans how to live, what to do or not to do, according to our own criteria. And most of the time we show little or no sensitivity toward the existing culture.'

Just then Paul returned from the market. Sensing the tension in the air, he decided to lighten things and suggested that we all join Anila and the children. I was impressed: in just a few hours they had already managed to clean the land of its brambles. All that remained to be done was a little more tilling, then planting, and presto! We'd turned what had been a desolate piece of overgrown property into a promising garden.

We treated ourselves to buttered tea and

some pancakes with mashed bananas while Kurt, still trying to prove that he too could work like the rest of us, was making a valiant effort to impress us out in the muddy field.

After fifteen minutes or so, however, he put down his shovel, brushed his clothes, and left. 'I lack your manual work experience,' he muttered, 'Some time I'll return to talk about working together!'

When a few days later, I ran into him on the Barkhor, he invited me to the Banak Shol. Since I always enjoyed visiting my old inn, I accepted. We sat on a wooden bench in his room.

'What's your decision about me?'

I realized he had no clue that he had irritated me, and that I had only been nice to him out of cowardice. We ordered banana lassi, an Indian drink made with yogurt.

'I just made an incredible discovery! That discovery will make me a millionaire! Since money means little to me — I am not a materialist — I want to invest some of my earnings in a worthwhile venture, like your school, for example. In exchange for this, will you hire me?'

'In what capacity, may I ask?'

'As a psychotherapist!'

'And precisely what would be the role of a psychotherapist in our school? I really don't need one. Nor do the children. Their priority is learning how to read and write.'

'I could teach them all about my discovery! When I'm rich and famous, you'll be proud to tell people I taught in your school!'

'What exactly is your discovery?'

'It has to do with energy of the unconscious,' he said in a less sure voice. 'Thanks to years of intense meditation, I have succeeded in unknotting the kinks of my brain. That energy' — Kurt paused dramatically — 'that energy is so powerful it can fuse electrons!'

'No kidding! How so?'

'It's quite simple, really,' he said. 'All I need to do is make my subconscious concentrate on a given target.'

I had trouble keeping a straight face. 'Your discovery has more to do with nuclear research, no? It seems to me you should offer your services to some scientific institution. Or a nuclear research center.'

'I did. No one was interested.'

'I still don't see how your discovery applies to our school.'

'Isn't it obvious? My ability to make my subconscious concentrate and focus on a particular object will enable me to heal many illnesses. Thanks to me, the world will be freed of AIDS. And cancer!'

'Congratulations.' My voice was betraying impatience.

'My invention will also restore sight to the blind!'

This time, I burst out laughing. 'And that would put me out of a job, right? But never mind. In any case, thanks but no thanks. There just isn't a place for you in our school.'

'I guess our spiritual planes are not in harmony.'

'Not really, Kurt. It would be best that we both go about using our energies as we have up to now: You focus on fusing electrons, and I'll keep on teaching the braille alphabet.'

And that was the last I heard of Kurt.

20

Behind our buildings — both the orphanage and our school — stretched a big sprawling lawn. We figured it could easily be fenced in one day if we needed to. Lopsang had in mind to buy two or three cows so we could have our own milk and dairy products. I also wanted some horses; it was important to teach our children how to ride. Having gone on horseback throughout the country's hilly and often difficult paths the previous year, I came to the conclusion that for a blind person, horseback riding is the safest means of transport in Tibet.

The best place to find horses, we were told, was in Chila's native village. When Chila's father volunteered to help us find some good horses for a reasonable price, we accepted with delight. There was a problem though: once we had located our horses, there was no one to bring them back. The only solution was to go get the horses ourselves.

We decided to turn the journey into a fun project, tying it in with an excursion to the warm springs at Tidrum, near Chila's village. Paul and I would ride the horses back to school, while the children would be brought home safely by car. It seemed like a simple project. No sooner did we mention our forthcoming adventure to the children than they started jumping up and down with joy. We had to keep them placated for days.

Finally the promised day arrived. The children, all eager and carrying their knapsacks, were lined up in a row at dawn, in front of the school, impatiently waiting for the arrival of the driver, Tsering, who had been hired for our excursion the previous day.

A few days before my parents had flown in, and my father, who had adapted remarkably to the altitude and the schedule change, decided to accompany us. That our journey was taking us two thousand feet higher didn't seem to faze him in the least. I was greatly impressed.

At 8.00 A.M. sharp, Tsering arrived in his slightly dilapidated Chinese station wagon. After packing the rear of his wagon with fruit, pancakes, noodles, onions, various kinds of absorbent paper, thermoses filled with buttered tea, and several bottles of mineral water, the children — still overexcited — were chirping like a bunch of little birds. They climbed into the station wagon, tightly holding onto their respective backpacks. Anila had decided to stay behind, and as it turned out, that was a good thing. Our vehicle, such as it was, would have been too small for one more passenger. Palden and Chila — who immediately started singing — sat next to Tsering. Needless to say, neither was wearing a safety belt, such items being considered a luxury in Tibet. My father was squeezed between Paul, Tashi, and me. We all took turns holding Norbu, who couldn't sit still, and Tendsin, who as soon as we started the trip began throwing up.

Chila's mother had come to Lhasa to do some shopping, and was returning to her village with us. She was sitting in the back like a queen, on top of some boxes, next to Meto. Judging from all she had packed into the wagon, it seemed as if she had emptied every last store in Lhasa of its baskets.

Meanwhile, the water level of the Kichu River had risen alarmingly in the last few days, and as we were driving on a road parallel to the river, we noticed that its banks, already partly submerged, had in some places disappeared altogether. Our driver was voicing serious concerns about our return trip. 'Let's just get there,' I told him. 'We'll take one day at a time.'

We stopped for lunch in a Chinese restaurant, in Medrogonga — a small town situated between the monastic university of Ganden and Drigung. The children seemed surprisingly at ease with chopsticks, which they were using for the first time. I was amused by Paul's description of how well they ate their noodle and pork soup without a problem. Or almost. Chila and Tendsin were apparently rather elegant in handling the new instruments, whereas the others managed a bit more clumsily. As for Tashi, he had found the most expedient way by bringing his bowl to his mouth, where, with the help of the chopsticks, he shoveled the food in. The worst off was my poor father, who was terribly frustrated chasing each slippery noodle one by one with his chopsticks.

Our driver, who since the start of the trip had not stopped smiling, was displaying great patience with his young passengers. In fact, he seemed to really be enjoying our noisy little group. 'I much prefer transporting this cheerful lot to the usual tourists I drive around Tibet,' he confessed. 'The tourists always seem to find something to complain about.' He had spoken too soon.

Chila, taking the rearview mirror for a swing, promptly succeeded in breaking it. And Tashi, who despite numerous stops for everyone to go to the toilets, graced us by peeing in his pants, to our dismay. Oblivious to it all, Tsering was carrying on with his jokes, maintaining his steadfast cheerfulness through thick and thin.

Paul and I, on the contrary, had by this time lost our cool and all sense of humor. After the unending series of little catastrophes throughout the journey, the smiles had left our faces. We were worn out and very tense.

★　★　★

We arrived in Chila's village, dropped his mother off with her panoply of baskets, and stayed long enough to drink the buttered tea she offered us. We would return the next day to pick up Chila's father, who, it was agreed, would help us negotiate the purchase of a couple of horses.

As we pressed on in the direction of Tidrum, the road had become nothing but mud, fallen stones, and small rocks. We were still following the river, but its water was rushing by with such deafening force that one could see it was fast wiping out most of the remaining banks.

We felt grateful to have Tsering as our driver: despite the many often dangerous obstacles in the road, he still seemed in perfect control, driving with astonishing calm. Seemingly unfazed when the road suddenly seemed to have disappeared altogether, he kept on driving straight ahead as if this was perfectly normal. As for the passengers, we were thrown from right to left, then back again, which greatly amused the children, with the exception of Tendsin, who, leaning far out the window, was carsick.

Our vehicle had turned into a cacophony of wild singing — in chorus at times, or in counterpoint. Chila, whose pleasant voice had in the past often been pressed into service to entertain us, was dominating the pack, yelling at the top of his lungs. And despite his legendary patience, no longer able to stand the assault of the tremendous noise, Palden ended up yelling louder: 'Kha tsum!' (Shut up!).

The only one unperturbed by it all was my father. Sitting squeezed between Tashi and the door, he was surveying the scenery with delight, taking pictures now and then, or checking his map in a cheerful mood. He was clearly determined to take full advantage of his vacation. After trying unsuccessfully to juggle holding the map and snapping pictures at the same time, he finally folded the map and stuffed it into Tashi's hand.

We were all too tired, and too exasperated by the noise and general mayhem, to notice two highly improbable road companions engaged in an intense dialogue: an animated discussion was taking place between Tashi, speaking Tibetan, and my father, responding in German. The fact that neither understood the other didn't seem to matter. Whatever was being communicated, Tashi appeared more alert and lively than he ever had before. It was obvious they had become fast friends.

Up to now at the school, we had almost given up all hope of ever extracting three consecutive coherent words out of this pathologically shy little boy. And here he was, engaged in a flawless discourse! Up to now his eyes had been kept forcibly shut. Why did he want to cut himself from the world? I had always wondered. I made a mental note to work on that with him. Right now, however, he was completely transformed, definitely enjoying life. Each bump in the road made him scream with joy. The more we swerved and swayed, the more cheerful he became. But the other children were frightened by now; they had stopped singing and were holding on to their seats for dear life. Tashi, dear shy Tashi with his newly found self-confidence, was the only one left singing and telling jokes.

★ ★ ★

We arrived at Tidrum — a thermal spa, highly appreciated by Lhasa residents — before sunset. The road led us up to an elevated pass that plunged into a gorge surrounded by sheer cliffs. This spectacular landscape was dominated by twenty-thousand-foot-high mountains and a foaming waterfall rushing loudly down from the mountains. We were all stunned by the deafening sound the waterfall made.

At the crest of the cliff was a small convent run by nuns, who took care of the hot springs and rented flea-infested beds to tourists. Since we were ten, we had rented eight beds. Our four boys would share two double beds. It all seemed simple. Tashi had been thoroughly washed and given new clothes at the start of the trip. When we announced who would share beds with whom, it triggered a small revolution in the ranks.

'No! I won't share a bed with Tashi, never! He stinks too much!' Chila responded.

Norbu and Tendsin had all along showed great kindness to Tashi, and to my delight had sort of adopted the little boy, taking him by the hand at school, playing with him in the courtyard or in the garden, and often accompanying him to the toilet. On the other hand, Chila, who always said what was on his mind, wasn't unsparing of Tashi this time.

Since Tashi hadn't yet mastered the art of anticipating his toilet needs, Chila recommended that we place Tashi's bed right inside the toilet — it would make it easier for him, and avoid discomfort for the rest of us!

In the middle of my reassuring speech about Tashi's improved habits, assuring the others that Tashi would be sure to warn us before anything happened, an overpowering smell wafted over us. Leaning over to Tashi, Chila let out a loud laugh. 'Sure, he'll warn us! And where does this wonderful smell come from?'

A sense of defeat took hold of me. Apparently Tashi turned flaming red and closed his eyes for the remainder of the evening. As if that wasn't bad enough, adding to Tashi's humiliation, Chila began hitting him over the head, chanting, 'Tashi made his pants dirty! Tashi stinks! Tashi stinks!'

Paul and I yanked Chila angrily away from the boy. Tashi instantly retreated into his shell, returning to his old mute self, his new self-confidence gone in an instant. We would have to build it anew. Because of his gentle nature, we asked Tendsin to go over and sit next to Tashi.

Tendsin was a particularly sweet and social little fellow. Anytime a child needed something, he would go first to Tendsin before coming to us. When the children needed to go to the toilet in the middle of the night, it was to Tendsin they would turn, waking him up and asking that he accompany them, because they were afraid of the night demons! So much in demand was Tendsin that he asked permission to keep his clothes when going to bed. That way, he explained, he would always be ready and wouldn't have to dress and undress three times a night.

21

The rain had stopped the previous night, and Tsering was reasonably sure our return trip would be uneventful. In Tibet, almost as soon as a downpour stops, river levels quickly descend, and banks once again come into view. But the roads, covered as they were with thick blankets of mud, were extremely slippery, making them tricky for any vehicle, especially one with a full cargo of rambunctious children. Fortunately this hazardous passage soon turned into a laughing party. Each time the car got stuck in the mud, the children had to pile out and with all their tiny strength push the station wagon onto firmer ground.

It took us longer than expected, but a few hours after we had left we arrived in Chila's village, where we got straight down to the business at hand: the purchase of horses. The ones selected by Chila's father were light brown with a deeper brown mane. One was rather young — no more than three years old. Chila's uncle was asking a fortune for it, no doubt assuming, as do most Tibetans, that we were rich westerners. It took some explaining to make them understand that we were not at all rich, that we existed merely on grant and donation money — which wasn't easy to come by.

'I have a large family to feed,' the uncle whined, 'not to mention my blind grandmother. The family is very attached to this good, obedient horse. To separate ourselves from such a horse would break all our hearts!'

All of which left me cold; I had learned better since my arrival.

After a good hour to-ing and fro-ing, he ended up coming down to a more reasonable price. Bargaining further, we even asked him to throw in the saddle, a full harness, and a sack of *tsampa* to feed the animal on the way back, all of which he finally agreed to.

We also bought from Chila's father a seven-year-old mare that looked well taken care of, with a nice shiny coat. All in all, we thought we had done pretty well: we had bought our two horses for the price of one, saddle, harness, and *tsampa* sacks included.

Palden, my father, and the children had already left for home in the station wagon before Paul and I began our return trip on horseback. Our horses were galloping merrily and obediently along, following the road until, at one point, despite all our efforts, they suddenly both turned onto a side road. We figured they must be heading for their usual grazing ground. As quick on their legs as mountain goats, they nimbly climbed the narrowest, rockiest paths, oblivious to any possible danger. All our valiant efforts to bring them back down were in vain. They were determined to stay on their familiar grass patch; nothing we could do changed that.

After they had finished grazing, these unpredictable mountain horses were now staging some kind of strike, simulating vertigo and shivering. Agitated and completely uncooperative, they rejected all our injunctions to move on. It took the longest time and a great deal of coaxing, cajoling, and encouraging shouts — not to mention infinite patience — to make our temperamental horses finally take the path leading us back down. No sooner had we breathed a sigh of relief when a new obstacle rose: a little gurgling spring, so narrow, gentle, and unobtrusive a dog could have crossed it. Having just conquered our horses' obstinacy, and their vertigo, we were now faced with a new problem: an acute and unexpected water phobia.

Unmoved by their new little act, and with impatience and authority this time, I succeeded in making my recalcitrant mare cross the water. Paul's horse, on the other hand, was less responsive, and I waited for what seemed like forever on the other side of the bank.

Despite our fatigue and a slow pace, we made it to the next village by the end of the afternoon. Starved, we found an eating place that served us some delicious Chinese roasted goat. While we were enjoying our meal, several villagers came over to us and offered to mind our horses — a very lovely Tibetan custom of hospitality we had already learned to appreciate throughout our trip.

Energized and refueled, we mounted and pushed on into the sunset, aiming to find the right spot in a meadow to pitch our tent. Paul opted for a patch of grass surrounded by a stone wall: it would be a quiet place for us to sleep, he promised, and we would be better protected from horse thieves than out in the open. To reach that perfect spot, however, we needed to climb a steep incline. And that posed a problem for our temperamental animals. As if they understood that this one last effort would bring them to our final destination, our testy and tired horses changed their minds and decided to climb, showing none of their previous fear. At the bottom of our wall-enclosed meadow, we could hear the loud sound of the famous warm spring, rushing down.

It was a cold, still night, and the sky was full of stars. We pitched our tent and fell asleep to the neighing of our horses, the tinkling of their bells, and the rushing water at the end of the meadow.

It was also Paul's birthday. He was thirty. In Holland — Paul's native country — when a man reaches thirty and is still unmarried, he is referred to as a 'beef,' he told me. While birthdays meant little to Paul, he told me, he nonetheless made three wishes: the first wish was for a lovely, sunny next day; the second, that our horses would behave; and the third — the most important one — that we find a television set the next evening so he could watch the World Cup. If the first two wishes were those of an optimist, his last one was definitely absurd! Where would we ever find a television in this forsaken desert?

We were awakened early next morning by smiling village women surrounding us, bearing a big hot thermos of water. We were no doubt an intriguing sight, and they were looking forward to sharing breakfast with us. We obliged, thanking them profusely, after which we climbed back on our horses. The sun was shining brightly, and the horses galloped peacefully along without any encouragement on our part. So far, both Paul's first two wishes had come true. Around noon, Paul's horse gave signs of fatigue, straying off the path. I had to wait for quite sometime for them to catch up with me.

We decided to go the rest of the way on foot and give our animals a rest. We passed some villagers working in the field along the way, who assured us that Medrogonga — the nearest village — was no more than two hours away.

'Not with *our* horses!' I said.

I couldn't have been more right. The sun had been beating down all day, and the horses were dehydrated and dead tired. The slightest obstacle, would make them stop in their tracks, only starting up again when they felt like it. Once again our journey, as it had been the previous day, turned into a game of cajoling and coaxing.

About six miles out of Medrogonga, Paul decided to dismount and walk the rest of the way, pulling his horse behind him. We arrived at the village five hours later — not two. Paul's hands were lacerated and bleeding.

Tired and more than slightly demoralized, we were slowly walking the main street when all of a sudden, out of nowhere, a huge gust of wind enveloped us in a cloud of sand and garbage. We somehow managed to attach the horses to a stout tree — hoping it would shield them from the sudden assault — and took refuge in a restaurant.

As was always the case, as soon as we were able to rest and eat some food, we were in a much better mood. Exploring the village, we found a room for a few yuan in a small inn. Paul, determined to have his thirtieth-birthday wish come true, asked the man at the inn to wake him up: he would find a way, somewhere, somehow, to watch his soccer game. He had no idea where, but he had made it his mission to find a place, no matter what, no matter how. Exhausted, we both crashed and fell into a deep sleep. In the middle of the night, our wake-up call came, in the shape of a young boy shaking Paul with all his might. Totally out, and clearly not understanding a word the boy was saying to him in Chinese, Paul didn't budge until the boy started singing the famous soccer hymn 'Go, go, go, olé, olé, olé!' which brought Paul immediately to his feet.

'You're crazy! Don't you know where we are? In the middle of nowhere!' I told Paul.

'I want to at least give it a try,' Paul said. We got dressed, and like two sleepwalkers, we wandered out in the night until, lo and behold! Paul located a small shop where a few Tibetans, squatting down in front of a minuscule black-and-white television set, were waiting for the match to begin.

Paul was in heaven, and it didn't matter that this was the middle of the night. He was reconciled with the whole world, including our crazy horses, who were neighing in the courtyard. This delightful, fanatic, and obsessed soccer fan miraculously had his third birthday wish, on the far side of the world, fulfilled.

* * *

By morning the previous evening's menacing clouds had given way to a deep blue sky, which promised us a beautiful, sunny day. Happy, if only partially rested, we started off with new energy, ready to face any obstacle along our way. The riverbanks had been swept away in many places, and worried, we had no choice but to cross waterfalls several times.

The night must have erased all previous fears our horses had harbored about water, for now they were crossing whatever rivers we came to without a whimper.

It was well into the evening when the village we were trying to reach finally appeared on the horizon. We asked a villager for some water. He called to another villager, who called to another, and before we knew it, we found ourselves surrounded by forty curious people. While in the past such crowds have often unnerved me, this time, having traveled twenty-five difficult miles on a very difficult horse, I was in no mood for small talk. I felt stifled. And, to top it all, two young Chinese girls pointed at me, commanding: 'Hey you, look over here!'

I didn't react and continued to feed the horses. That imperious and uncalled-for order was followed by a number of derogatory comments aimed at me: 'Forget it! This girl's an idiot! She can't even look when spoken to!'

That did it! Suddenly all the memories of primary school came flooding back, my schoolmates always laughing behind my back, constantly leading me to places where they knew I would stumble and fall.

'Look here,' the Chinese girls yelled. 'I guess she doesn't have any eyes! What an idiot!'

'This way! Look over here!' a chorus of young Tibetans chimed in, waving their smelly fingers, which reeked of rancid butter, in front of my eyes. The circle of people — adults and children — was closing in on me. Where was Paul when I needed him? He had left me to feed the horses while he explored the village. Now, alone, I was overcome with panic; all I wanted to do was leave as fast as I could. As if he had read my mind, Paul suddenly appeared, and the villagers' tone suddenly changed from menacing to friendly. Paul was, after all, six foot two, and very fit. He had found a villager who was willing to take us in but then had suddenly remembered that taking in foreign travelers was not such a good idea. I breathed a sigh of relief, for I remembered our agonizing night with the fleas and rats. In any case, he had directed Paul to an open field near a river, where we could pitch our tent.

Paul announced he would take the horses and the baggage up to the field first. But, having had my fill of intimidation and humiliation, I had no intention of staying behind.

'Why not?' Paul asked. 'It isn't the first time we've drawn a crowd.' Paul still couldn't understand why I was so upset. Since he spoke neither Chinese nor Tibetan, he had no idea what had happened. In fact, they were starting in again. 'I tell you, she's got to be a complete idiot! Otherwise she'd be looking at us!' someone was saying.

Enough was too much!

'*You're* the idiots!' I shouted. 'Isn't it obvious to you I can't *see!*'

The fact that the 'idiot' was answering

them in their native tongue made no impression on them.

'You can't? Why don't you go see a doctor?' someone offered.

'Is that why you're wearing these funny eyeglasses?' chimed in another.

I realized my skiing goggles must have made me look especially strange to them.

This ugly incident was partially offset by a kind villager, who offered to take care of our horses for the night.

We pitched our tent under the gaze of half the village, who watched in amazement as we blew up our pneumatic mattresses and unrolled our sleeping bags.

At dusk, our 'audience' finally disappeared, leaving us finally to catch a well-deserved rest.

The clucking of chickens, followed by the cries and shouts of children, woke us up good and early the next morning. Looking around, we saw that our camping site was once again bustling with people. We drank our tea and quickly packed our gear. The villager who had offered to take care of our horses had brought them back to us with full bellies and helped us load up.

'What is your next stop?' someone asked. When I said 'Lhasa!' they broke out laughing, as though I had said, 'The moon.'

'It'll take you at least two days to get there, unless you travel through the night!' one person offered. With that encouragement in mind, we started out on our journey.

By the end of the afternoon, we found ourselves traveling on the main road, only a dozen miles from Lhasa. The horses of course had never been on a paved road, and of course, right on cue, they stopped dead, frightened by the unfamiliar surface. Patiently coaxing them on, we finally managed to convince them to proceed, one step at a time. It took a while before they accepted this concrete surface — this miracle of modern times.

Cars were now passing us at great speed in both directions, and discretion being the better part of valor, we dismounted and continued pulling our horse by the reins.

'We're only one and half miles from the army barracks,' Paul announced encouragingly. 'Two miles farther, and we'll be on the bridge leading to Lhasa!'

The barracks came and went, and still there was no bridge in sight. Night was falling, cars had put on their headlights, and traffic was becoming increasingly dangerous.

'How far is the bridge to Lhasa?' we asked a group of soldiers driving by.

'Ten miles!' they answered in chorus.

233

'Tibetans don't have any sense of distance,' Paul muttered. It turned out it was he who didn't. It turned out the bridge *was* a good ten miles away.

Stumbling on the smallest stone on the road, our horses were advancing slowly when a strong wind came up, enveloping us once again in all sorts of garbage and dust. Paul did his best to fend off the sandstorm and onslaught of flying plastic bags, to no avail. Stones were hitting us everywhere, making such a noise, it was impossible for me to hear. Had I been a horse, I thought, I would certainly have bucked. But to our surprise, at this critical moment our unpredictable animals continued bravely on. The wind died down, quickly replaced by rain, which cooled things down considerably.

Soaked to my skin, with my teeth chattering, I decided it was my turn to go on strike. I was ready to sit down at the edge of the road for the rest of the night and fall asleep. In fact, sleeping was all I could think of.

Paul convinced me to remount, which I did with great reluctance: I was freezing and no longer had any feeling in my hands or feet. After a while I dismounted again. Wading through more endless puddles and heaps of garbage for what seemed like several more hours, we reached our destination. In a state of total exhaustion, drenched to the bone, and starved, we at long last reached the gate of the school. It was one o'clock in the morning. The concierge, who was still awake, couldn't believe his eyes at the sight of us: two more miserable-looking creatures would have been hard to imagine.

What had started off as a lark, a fun-filled two-day journey on horseback, had turned into an endless odyssey. No, a nightmare.

22

Some time later, when we were fully recovered and our return to Lhasa only a fading memory, a warm and sunny day inspired us to hold our class outdoors in the courtyard. Our neighbors — the children from the orphanage, curious to see what their blind schoolmates were up to — ran up and watched with fascination as our kids read with their fingers and wrote with little circles of felt.

I had entrusted Norbu — the first to have mastered braille Tibetan characters — to show the class how to use the little wooden boards, the adhesive squares and felt circles. He was by far the most intelligent of the class, and he loved performing. Now that he had been given an official and important role in front of a class eager to listen, though, he suddenly turned shy. Huddling behind his desk, refusing to move, he protested in a barely audible voice, 'But I don't know anything!' It was Meto, the 'old one' — she was all of twelve — who took things in hand.

Facing her audience, she ordered the orphans to sit up and stop talking, and began teaching all the children — she knew the method.

Both the blind and the orphans responded with enthusiasm, clapping. First, she made them sing in chorus. Then they had to recite the alphabet, one after the other. When the class was over, the orphans asked Palden, who had observed his new 'teacher's' performance, if they could always have class together, with *all* the children, blind or not. It was a logical outcome, and pleased me no end. Our objective was integration as soon as possible; our ultimate aim to return our little blind pupils to their respective village schools. This experiment encouraged us. We could see the possibilities for a future integrated program, but we knew there were all sorts of inherent problems.

Out of nowhere Chungda suddenly appeared at my side. After watching Meto in her new role for a few minutes, she pulled me aside.

'I need to speak to you. One on one!' she said. I did not like her tone. In any case we repaired to an empty classroom, where Chungda carefully closed the doors and windows.

'What's up?' I asked, surprised by her conspiratorial tone.

'Paul,' she said. 'I don't want Paul mixing

himself in the affairs of the orphanage anymore!' I was taken aback by her hostility. Up to now, she had seemed enchanted by Paul's involvement; in fact, she was constantly seeking his company, constantly asking his advice about her computer.

'What happened? Has he been impolite?' I asked.

'No, no. I simply want you to ask him to stop doing our accounting. Immediately.'

'Why? I don't get it. I thought he was such a help to you — '

'He sticks his nose in places that are none of his business!' she interrupted, this time with rage in her voice. She left the classroom, slamming the door behind her.

In a state of shock, I walked over to the office where Paul worked. Hadn't she been the one who wanted and really appreciated Paul's computer expertise? Accounting, she had said, was easy; all Chungda needed was Paul's help in straightening a few things out.

'What happened?' I asked him.

'I did have a slight altercation with Chungda when I picked up something fishy in her accounting. Sabriye, none of the book entries correspond to the real numbers. Let me give you one example: all the employees' salaries are entered at a higher amount than the salary actually paid them. Unilaterally

Lopsang decided that giving different salaries to people who work and live under the same roof was not a good idea.

'Right from the start, it had been he who had worked out the salary scale: a teacher for the blind was to earn a thousand yuan a month — roughly $100 — whereas a regular teacher, such as those at the orphanage, was paid only two hundred yuan. These salary disparities struck me as odd, especially considering that an average salary in Tibet is five hundred to seven hundred yuan per year. Anyway, relying on Lopsang's presumed expertise, I had explained the disparity to the German ministry: that those teaching the blind require more training, hence the higher pay.'

How was it possible that Lopsang had not put into practice his principles? I was confused to say the least, and upset. I knew we now had plenty of money in the coffers. We had twice received funds from Germany, and when my parents arrived, they had, as promised, brought the sum I had asked for out of my personal account. What was more, my affiliated organization back home had finally come through with its promised funds. Lopsang had been visibly delighted when all that money had been transferred, and had assured me that from now on all would go smoothly.

But that wasn't all. Paul had uncovered another disturbing discrepancy: the account books showed money spent for furniture and other items that had never been given to the school. For instance, at one point I had asked that a safe be built in my desk for storing important documents. The purchase of the safe had indeed been entered, but no safe had ever been delivered to me.

'Yes,' Chungda admitted sheepishly, 'there is a problem with that safe. It's here all right,' she said, tapping on the windowpane, 'but unfortunately we can't give it to you. You see, we can't open the safe — we somehow lost the key.'

My face must have shown disbelief, because she immediately added, 'You would understand if only you could see!'

Paul decided to verify this story. He went to the warehouse and looked through all the windows, walked all around, and looked some more. He came away without ever having seen most of what had been entered as 'paid-for' furniture in the ledger. The few pieces he did end up locating were totally insignificant, and even so were entered in the ledger at inflated prices. Paul had seen similar pieces in Lhasa for half the price noted in the books.

'We decided to purchase the school furniture for you, because, you know, foreigners so often get ripped off!' Chungda's words came flashing back to me. Either Lopsang and Chungda had been had by the furniture shop where they bought that table, or ... I didn't want to contemplate the alternative.

'Did you bring all this up with her?' I asked Paul, more and more upset.

'When I asked her to get a couple of strong men to help me carry the furniture to the school, she simply replied, 'There is no furniture!' '

'No furniture? Not even in the *warehouse?*' I asked meekly.

'I was as surprised as you,' Paul said. 'But just listen to her lame answer: 'What's in the warehouse are broken, damaged, and unusable pieces!' she said. When I offered to try and repair them, she flew into a rage. 'It's none of your business, Paul,' she said. 'Keep your nose out of it!' By now, she knows I've found them out.'

The embezzlement scheme involved everything, across the board. I could function very well without an armoire or a bookcase, for that matter. What was infinitely more important was the fact that our children had no mattresses, nor were there any sheets to change on the beds. The kids had been sleeping directly on the wooden springs, with only thin blankets to keep them from the cold. Here, too, Paul had seen in the account books expenses relating to the purchase of mattresses and sheets.

I was thunderstruck, unable to say a word for the longest time. What an appalling situation! Why hadn't Anila and Palden told me about any of this? Why hadn't they described the state of the dormitory to me? I had lived in the peaceful certitude that finally we were well provided for, financially secure, when in fact things had only gotten worse. Terribly worse . . .

Paul and I decided to remain calm and not confront Chungda yet; we needed advice. We went to consult some colleagues who, like us, were working in various humanitarian organizations in Lhasa. They too, it turned out, had made similar mistakes in letting the locals help run their organizations. But having learned the hard way, they advised us, it was imperative we run our own project. Equally imperative: we needed to hire a competent outside accountant.

I wasted no time in requesting an immediate meeting with Lopsang. I told him unequivocally that, in the case of projects funded by foreign money such as ours, extreme competence in bookkeeping was mandatory — implying in a veiled way that accounting errors would be dealt with severely. I demanded that Paul have full charge of our books from now on. He voiced no objection, saying he'd be happy to comply on the condition that he receive a fax from our German organization confirming all this. The fax nominating Paul as our official bookkeeper/accountant arrived the next day.

Needless to say, when Chungda got wind of all this, she threw a tantrum.

'What, may I ask, is this?' she yelled, crumpling up the fax into a ball and throwing it down at Paul's feet.

'Oh, nothing, except that from today on I'm the one who will take full charge of our bookkeeping. Furthermore, our school will open its own bank account, and our foreign funds will go directly there.'

'And as for you, my dear,' Paul went on unctuously, 'it will mean far less work.'

'All it says to me,' she retorted, 'is that with this method you'll do whatever you want with the money. A good way to get rich!'

And she left in a huff.

23

Word of mouth about our project and our school had traveled far afield. 'The very first school for the blind in Tibet' had become the subject of a great deal of international curiosity, and as a result we were besieged by journalists and documentary filmmakers from around the world. In Tibet however, no one is allowed to work — least of all journalists and members of foreign media — without the official permission of the government authorities. Truth be told, if the authorities had their way, all foreign journalists and filmmakers would be banned and sent packing across the border. Those who do manage to get here, to write or make a film in Tibet, generally are very well connected. Even so, they're still subject to all the intricacies of Tibetan bureaucracy. Actually, the most important element is arriving with a fat wallet.

In any event, one fine day a Scandinavian reporter named Ole showed up at our door, intent on making a filmed documentary on us and the school. He seemed nice enough, so we accepted. After spending some time filming the school itself, Ole agreed to meet us for a picnic in the Potala park on Sunday. Potala was graced with a big sports field and various kinds of entertainment, all of which would be fun for the children, but also provided Ole with some good material for his documentary.

That Sunday morning, while Paul and I were working in our respective offices, Ole entered, unannounced and out of breath.

'Sorry. I didn't come alone.'

'Really?' Paul said. 'Who did you bring with you?'

Embarrassed, Ole told us that authorities in Beijing had sent an 'escort' to accompany him wherever he went.

'She's very conscientious, follows my every step. Once a day, when she thinks I'm in my room, she calls someone — no idea who — and gives a daily report about me and my every move.'

'That's odd,' Paul said, frowning. 'The last time you came, you were alone! Where was she?'

'Well, that day I outsmarted her,' Ole said. 'While she thought I was in my room and she was giving her daily phone report, I sneaked out. Of course, the next day, she gave me holy hell and has been glued to me ever since. 'You Europeans are so hard to handle,' she told me, 'so unpredictable!' She's turned into a real watchdog. And this morning, I'm sorry to say, I couldn't shake her.'

Keenly aware of the unforgiving Chinese bureaucracy, we advised Ole not to do any filming that day. He was sorely disappointed, but agreed. Nevertheless, he slipped a small camera into his knapsack, 'Just in case . . . '

After gathering the children, we formally invited the watchdog to join us. It never hurts to be polite, I figured, and anyway, I knew she would be coming, invited or not.

The big game field, it turned out, was locked. Making the best of it, we guided our little troop over to the Chinese amusement park, with its bumper cars, loudspeakers, and a huge trampoline — where, for ten yuan, the children could jump to their heart's content. They were having a ball. Well, almost everyone: little Tashi was hanging onto us for dear life while Meto, Norbu, and Tendsin jumped merrily, screaming at the top of their lungs. In fact, our venerable school for the blind had for all intents and purposes monopolized the trampoline, preventing other children from climbing onto it and sending them, frustrated and crying, back into their mothers' arms. As for Chila, he seemed to have taken root in the trampoline, occupying the center of the canvas, oblivious of everything around him.

To boot, he was performing a little imitation juggling act, tossing little plastic balls, into the air.

Each time some sighted children tried to approach the trampoline, Chila could hear them, bombard them with his plastic balls, and chase them away, wailing, to their angry mothers. As much as it pleased me to know our outing was such a success, I was more than slightly embarrassed to draw this kind of negative attention to our group.

When Paul and Ole decided to join the trampoline party, the woman issuing tickets at the entrance protested loudly. Needless to say, the combination of these two presumed adults furiously jumping alongside our out-of-control blind children created quite a spectacle. A crowd had soon gathered around the trampoline, sharing the fun and general hilarity.

Meanwhile, overcome by this latest development, I stood helpless between Anila and Ole's Chinese agent, who, understandably, did not especially appreciate the unexpected sideshow.

Our mad jumping group soon reached a point of complete exhaustion, and to the relief of everyone most of Lhasa's population, I was certain — finally liberated the trampoline. Looking forward to a much-needed moment of peace and quiet, I led my little group deeper into the park and picked a spot in a rolling meadow for our picnic. But no sooner had we started taking the food out of our baskets and handing it out to the children than a cloud of hungry pigeons flew over us, targeting our food. For our already overexcited kids, this latest adventure seemed a perfect excuse to scream and chase the pigeons away — followed shortly, of course, by our two no less mad adult men.

Resigned that there was nothing, simply nothing, I could do, I stayed put on our blanket with Anila, two of the boys, and our friend's Chinese agent, who by now had abdicated and temporarily given up her watchdog mission. Sensing which, Ole didn't waste a moment. Taking full advantage of this unexpected reprieve, he pulled his camera out of his knapsack and quickly began filming our little pack running in mad confusion after the birds.

'These are maybe the most beautiful pictures I've ever filmed,' he gushed, 'thank you, thank you! A great scene! Norbu, Meto, and Tendsin in a wild dance with pigeons, against a stunning backdrop of Tibetans jumping up and down with loud cheers. Wonderful!'

Ole's very positive visit suddenly reminded

me of a reporter-photographer from a European magazine who had come to see us a year earlier, intent on capturing 'lively, human, moving' pictures of us and the school. His name was Angello, a name that for me will live in infamy. When the magazine's editor in chief originally contacted me, asking my permission for Angello to interview and photograph us, I had agreed, keeping in mind that any effort to inspire eventual investors, wherever they might be, was all to the good.

For a long time we had planned a school excursion that included the children from the orphanage. Though it didn't exactly fit Angello's original story concept, he resigned himself to the outing.

We all left early one morning, heading for the old Buddhist university of Ganden, taking time, on top of the sacred mountain, to visit the small chapels and the temple of Ganden, all virtually destroyed during the Cultural Revolution and only recently rebuilt. Concerned the pictures would be of little use, Angello suggested a scenario in which I, along with the children, would climb out on the rickety roof of an old chapel.

'Great idea,' I said. 'Why don't I jump off the roof while you're at it, just to keep your viewers' interest?'

He apologized, and did no further shooting that day.

The next morning, armed with all his equipment, Angello arrived at the school, to take pictures of our classes in full progress.

Meanwhile our neighbors, the children from the orphanage, intrigued and curious about Angello and his impressive photographic equipment, had tiptoed to join our children in the classroom.

'All these kids! Perfect! They'll make a colorful group for my photos!' Angello exclaimed.

Palden and I were to conduct our class, oblivious of his presence. Not easy, really. Each time I paid special attention to one of the children, Angello would rush over, making me freeze for a few minutes — while admonishing me not to become self-conscious — so he could take a 'meaningful' photograph. Or, worse, he would ask me to turn Tendsin's head toward the camera, demanding that he either look down or up toward the ceiling, each time making the poor child keep that particular pose for the longest time. Poor little Tendsin couldn't understand what was going on. Frankly I couldn't either. I had naively thought that for such a documentary a photographer would want to take candid pictures of us in action, in our natural daily lives. Finally I told Angello I had no intention of giving our children a stiff neck for the sake of his magazine. Apparently he wasn't used to having his subjects argue with him, so he was slightly miffed. When recess rang, Angello was further irritated as all the orphans ran like bats out of hell into the courtyard. Recess was sacred!

'What do you think you're doing?' he exclaimed. 'You can't all just leave in the middle of my work!'

I burst out laughing. 'First of all, these children don't understand a word you're saying. Second, it's recess; they all look forward to it, it's their time to play. And the same applies for my children too, as a matter of fact.'

'You don't seem to understand the pressure I'm under, my dear,' Angello said patronizingly. 'My magazine has gone to a great deal of trouble, *and* spent a small fortune, to send me halfway across the world. In exchange, they expect pictures with a *punch*, an exciting story line. I count on your cooperation.'

He's right, I thought. I had agreed to let him come to photograph us for his magazine. I had no choice but to cooperate. I asked Anila for once to serve the children their tea in the classroom, so Angello could continue his photo shoot uninterrupted despite the loss of the orphans. He had already taken a great number of pictures — well over a hundred, as far as I could judge — when the door of our classroom suddenly burst open, and in marched fifteen soldiers, quickly surrounding us. I froze with fear. What was happening? What were they here for? Pulling me aside, Angello whispered nervously, 'Do you think it's because of *me?*'

'No, I can't imagine why they're here,' I replied. But suddenly I wondered whether he had come to Tibet with the necessary accreditations and permissions.

With my usual foreigner's paranoia, but pretending to make the best of the situation, I pointed to the children's blackboards, hoping to demonstrate to the soldiers that we were here on a legitimate mission, with no ulterior political motive. Breaking into Chinese, I went about explaining to the soldiers the principles of braille. To my surprise, they seemed to be greatly interested, even rather friendly. And a few minutes later they departed. Their intrusion, I was later told, was routine; a high-ranking government personality was expected in the area, and their visit to our school was a mere security measure.

A bit undone by this unexpected arrival, I gave everyone a short break and repaired to my office. I hadn't been there two minutes when I heard Angello's voice from the courtyard: 'Stop! I don't want to be photographed!' he shouted.

I rushed out.

'What's the problem, Angello? Who is photographing you?' I asked.

'This guy did!' He pointed to Lopsang.

'This 'guy,' my friend, happens to be the school's director. As long as you take pictures of our school, he feels entitled to do the same with you. I see nothing wrong with that!'

I was suddenly fed up with Angello and his whole interview and felt a strong urge to toss him out on his western ear. He must have sensed my anger, for in a subdued voice, he asked to take only a few more pictures of Paul and me. Once again, I mastered my seething anger and let him photograph us.

His next wish for his 'punchy documentary' was to photograph the founder of the school for the blind — me — on horseback, riding through the Tibetan mountains. I asked Penda, my stable boy, to fetch my horse and tack it up for me. He brought me Paul's mare — which we had baptized Pungu, 'donkey' in Tibetan. Pungu was not only stubborn, she could also have tantrums like a goat, especially when she was taken away from Lhamo, the mare she considered her mother. Right on cue, knowing Lhamo had stayed behind in the meadow grazing peacefully, Pungu tried to bite us when we put on the bridle. That suited Angello just fine. Why should he care? For his assignment, it was great to photograph a blind Amazon dealing with her challenging horse. Resigned, I mounted the angry mare, whose only desire, I knew, was to throw me off. Predictably, she bucked, raced away, jumped over a ravine filled with water — something she would normally never have attempted — and galloped straight toward the meadow where her adoptive mother was grazing. Delighted by this mini-drama, Angello was clicking away, all the while yelling, 'Terrific! Now can you come back toward me?'

Meanwhile I was hanging on for dear life, saying to myself, 'To hell with all magazines and photographers in the world!' Probably sensing my rage, the mare calmed down, turned around, and raced back in the direction of Angello and all his equipment. Poor Angello barely had time to jump aside to avoid being trampled. After this escapade, Pungu stopped dead beside him as if nothing had happened.

During this whole little episode, the orphanage children had gathered and formed a cluster, following the spectacle and punctuating each move with a loud, happy shout. Aware that most of them were excellent riders, I couldn't help but be ashamed of my inability to keep Pungu under control.

Eager to be a part of this circus, the children had formed a circle around the mare. As for Angello, he was getting more and more excited at the thought of all the 'interesting' pictures he was unexpectedly getting.

Pungu was nervously edging away, looking ready to buck and bite any intruder. Angello, undeterred by anything, asked a little girl from the orphanage to stand next to me and hold my hand.

In the meantime, as we all played our respective roles as models and photographer, none of us had noticed that one of the boys behind me was positioning himself to jump onto Pungu, which he did, landing right next to me on the saddle. Pungu was so startled that, in a desire to rid herself of all these irksome children — and me, no doubt — she took off, heading straight toward a pile of rubble. I knew the terrain there was very rocky, and if I fell off Pungu, I would surely fracture something. Holding on tight, I made up my mind to make a wild effort to stay in the saddle, no matter what.

Pungu jumped over the pile and landed on

the other side, safe and sound — with me still seated firmly in the saddle. I breathed a deep sigh of relief. The swampy meadow, surrounded by a few trees and very high mountains, would have been precisely what Angello appreciated. Too bad he hadn't followed us: this dramatic landscape would surely have provided the final 'splendid' picture he had been looking for.

I must have looked pale and disheveled by the time I reached my office; my mother took one look at me and urged me to go lie down. Angello's job wasn't finished, though. He wanted one more picture of Paul and me at our respective desks. Thinking that was the only way to get rid of him, we obliged.

Preparing to take his leave, Angello thanked us and confessed how relieved he was not to have had any run-in with the authorities. 'When those soldiers marched into the school, I thought my goose was cooked,' he admitted.

'Why?' I inquired.

After a moment's hesitation, he said sheepishly, 'Well, I might as well tell you now, I entered Tibet on a tourist visa. But don't worry about me, I'll get the film out all right.'

Hearing this, Paul and I were livid. And like Pungu, we too bucked.

'We, worry about you! You can't be serious

It's our school we're worried about. Do you know you put us all at risk? If the authorities had known, you would have jeopardized our school, even our entire future in Tibet!'

'For goodness sake, calm down!' Angello said. 'No one will ever take exception to all this!'

Wrong. Someone did take exception. That same evening, Palden informed us that Paul's and my visas were not going to be renewed. Furthermore, we were ordered out of the country. Immediately!

24

It had all begun after Angello's stunning confession.

When I informed Lopsang of this latest development, he wasted no time in telling us that he no longer had any interest in our school for the blind. 'You've become a liability,' he said. 'Clearly you've committed some error that forced the authorities to expel you. You'd better leave as soon as possible,' he advised, not even trying to be diplomatic. 'Go to Kathmandu and apply for a new visa. I don't know what more to suggest!'

'As for you, Paul,' Chungda chimed in, 'I think it would be a good idea if you never set foot in our country again!'

'Thanks for the advice,' Paul said tartly, 'but I'm as much of this project as Sabriye is. I have no intention of turning my back on it.'

To be thrown out of a country where we thought we were building something worthwhile was horribly depressing. That evening I was sitting on a low stone wall, totally demoralized, when Paul came over and sat down next to me. Putting his arms around me, he said, 'It's all going to work out,

Sabriye, you'll see! Tomorrow we'll go to the foreign affairs desk, and I'm sure we'll get our visas renewed right there. We won't even have to leave the country.'

Next morning, bright and early, we went from office to office at the ministry of foreign affairs, to no avail. Everywhere the answer was the same: 'Sorry, but here in Lhasa there's nothing we can do for you. To request a reentry visa you have to go to Nepal.'

After our third turndown, even Paul began to lose faith, his innate optimism doing a fast fade.

We were painfully aware that leaving our children at this crucial stage was terrible. Our program was much too young; no one was experienced enough to take over. Who would take care of the children? Anila was an excellent administrator, and we knew how devoted she was to our little charges. But she, like Palden, was fainthearted: in the event of any problems with Lopsang, neither one would be capable of confronting or opposing him. And what about our bookkeeping? Our money? There was always Dolma, of course. She was both able and fully worthy of our trust. Anila and the children both knew her well. But Dolma was currently away on one of her medical missions and wouldn't be back 'n Lhasa for another month. No one could reach her, not even by phone, to let her know what had happened to us. I was in a state of despair when I heard a voice shining in the darkness.

'If you're looking for someone to help take care of the school, I'd be only too pleased to,' my mother was saying.

She had listened to all our lamentations and decided to step in. My father had been obliged to fly back to Germany a few days before, she told me, but she had been quite taken by Tibet and, she insisted, had decided to stay on a bit longer anyway. She wanted to read, wander a bit along the banks of Banak Shol — in short, play the tourist. Her offer to pitch in altered her original plans, but she didn't mind a bit.

'You mustn't worry,' she insisted. 'I'll handle everything. And to boot, I know I'll really enjoy it.'

How blessed I am to have such parents, who have the rare and wonderful quality of always being there when I need them.

★ ★ ★

A few days later, en route to the Nepalese border, Paul and I had taken off in a four-wheel-drive station wagon. The rainy season was upon us, and tourists were rightly worried about the catastrophic condition of the roads. All planes were fully booked, however, and we had no choice but to go by car if we wanted to get out of the country fast. We called on the same driver, Tsering, who had taken such good care of us earlier. The road on which we were traveling — called the Friendship Highway, and considered one of Tibet's best — was unrecognizable, already covered with the debris of fallen rock, virtually buried under a mountain of mud. In fact, in places the road had turned into a veritable waterfall as more rain gushed down the slopes. Here and there trucks and other vehicles had simply been left on the road, while several tourists, obliged to abandon their vehicles, were on foot, dragging their luggage toward the nearest village. Our vehicle, it turned out, was the last to reach the Nepalese border before the onset of the rainy season, thanks especially to Tsering, who seemed to overcome every obstacle we encountered with the greatest of ease. Luckily, I was blissfully unaware of all this, Paul having scrupulously avoided giving me any description of the awful road conditions. During the most dangerous moments he fooled me by yawning, telling me how bored he was.

We had arrived at a point in our journey

where we had no choice but to cross a river. In any case, the bridge was out, so we faced three possible solutions, Tsering told us candidly: 'The first is to turn back, the second, to sprout wings and fly over, and the third, take a risk and cross it!' Most of the other drivers, he warned us, had opted for the first solution. When Paul showed him our expiring visas, he understood. 'All right,' he said. 'Let's go for the third.' And gunning the motor, praying, we pushed across the water. Tsering knew that staying in Tibet with an expired visa meant a serious fine.

I had no idea how dangerous the passage was. All I could hear was our engine growling as waves beat against the windows. If the engine had died in the middle of the stream, we would doubtless have been swept away by the strong current. As we arrived safely on the other side, we found the road blocked: a team of dynamiters was in the process of removing a rock as big as a house that had fallen on the road, smashing a car to smithereens and killing all its occupants.

From Lhasa, it normally only took two days to reach the Nepalese border town of Zhangmu, Tsering told us. It had taken us four.

A typical little Chinese-Tibetan border town, Zhangmu was ugly, poor, and dirty, its muddy streets strewn with cans of Coke, empty cigarette packs, and plastic bags. A mixture of boredom, indifference, and poverty reigned supreme despite the loudspeakers planted throughout the town, which blared loud music, interrupted now and again by speeches.

We arrived with only one desire in mind: to leave this dreadful little place behind as fast as we could. But as luck would have it, the customs office had just closed for the day, only ten minutes earlier. 'Too late! Sorry!' a Chinese customs official informed us. Waving our expired visas, Paul implored him, to no avail. The customs official pointed to a hotel where we could spend the night. Strange situation — thrown out of Tibet on the one hand, we couldn't get past the border because the men were going home.

The hotel was dirty and expensive, but, exhausted both physically and emotionally, we were grateful for a place to sleep. The next morning we returned to the border checkpoint. After much pleading, Tsering managed to talk the men into stamping our passports, even though our visas had expired the day before, sparing us a stiff penalty. Tsering — the best driver in all of Tibet, in our opinion — bid us good-bye. He could not drive us any farther; the roads in this no-man's land had become impassable because of the rock avalanches. We were more than sorry to see him go.

Knapsacks on our backs, we walked the five miles separating us from the Friendship Bridge, which marks the actual border. This stretch was extremely dangerous and tiring. Loaded with heavy gear and wearing the wrong shoes, we had to climb over slippery rocks and wade through muddy rivers and rushing torrents. By the time we finally staggered across the bridge and crossed the red line between China and Nepal, we were two pitiful voyagers, our feet literally dragging.

As we crossed the symbolic divide, Paul turned back one last time. The Chinese soldiers in their pristine uniforms stared at us with disapproval, while in front of us, the Nepalese, seated on the edge of the bridge, their feet dangling in the air, smoked nonchalantly without a negative thought in their heads.

'Welcome to Nepal!' They greeted us with a big smile, and we were taken over to a cabin where we filled out some forms and other documents, and were even offered some tea.

We did indeed feel welcome. With a valid passport, a few dollars, and an identity photo it never takes more than ten minutes t obtain a visa in Nepal. No matter what transpires, their attitude seems to be; No problem.

Smiling at Paul, one of the functionaries pointed to his form: 'You have little problem!' Paul didn't have a photo, as requested in the form. With a malicious smile, he added; 'You give five dollars, then little problem is no problem.'

'Five dollars?' Paul asked.

Pulling a group photo out of his pocket, Paul cut the other people in the photo away, leaving only his head, and handed it to the border inspector. Laughing like a happy child, the man glued it onto the form.

'No problem!' he concluded.

But our trials and tribulations were far from over. The road to Kathmandu, we learned, was blocked in several places. The monsoon — particularly heavy these past few days — had caused several mudslides. We nevertheless managed to drag ourselves to the nearest village, where a truck was waiting to take travelers like ourselves to the Nepalese capital.

Squeezed between some twenty Nepalese, we were in such a state of exhaustion we wondered whether we would ever be able to stand up again when we reached Kathmandu. But our worries were for naught; our truck progressed no farther than the next mudslide.

Another huge rock had fallen, destroying a bridge spanning a raging river. Of the bridge only one thin plank remained, less than a foot wide, and forty feet long. Enough to get us across, someone assured us. I'm no tightrope walker, and though I can't see, I'm afraid of the void. I also knew there was no net, and the precarious wooden passage was roughly a hundred and fifty feet above the river. It was also far from certain that this plank of narrow, dubious wood would sustain our weights. But the sun was shining again now, and our cheerful travel companions did their best to reassure us that everything would be fine, that there was nothing unusual about any of this.

We inched ourselves slowly across. I wasn't proud. As soon as we had made it to the other side, someone confessed that the bridge had sagged dangerously under our weight as we went across.

'The worst is over!' Paul declared. He was being overly optimistic, for he knew what lay ahead. 'I think we've had enough for one day,' he said with a deep sigh a short while later.

★ ★ ★

A little farther on, we all piled into another truck, hoping to continue our lengthening journey. But once again the truck stopped dead at the edge of an abyss where, before the monsoon, there had been a road. All that was left was a steep incline filled with debris. We could either attempt climbing on foot or wait at least a week for the road to be cleared. The choice was simple. We simply *had* to try. A Nepalese man who seemed to have become our self-appointed leader, sensing how afraid everyone was, took our heavy knapsacks, which made it easier for us to climb the steep inclines.

Becoming used to great efforts, we managed, and once again made it to the other side, where a brand-new jeep belonging to a Chinese technician for Nepalese Hydraulic Works seemed to be waiting for us. This philanthropist had no objection when we spread ourselves, with our muddy clothes, on the superb, pristine seats of his vehicle. Appreciating the welcome reprieve, Paul quickly regained his good humor. 'The worst is over!' I heard him declare for the nth time.

Twenty minutes later, our luxurious ride came to an end. Another mudslide had removed the retaining wall of the road, and a mountain of earth and of mud had covered it, making it impossible for any vehicle to get through. The only way for us to (barely) continue was up another steep incline of slowly sliding mud, overhanging a precipice more than three hundred feet deep.

Once again friendly hands divested me of my knapsack, and a Nepalese had been appointed to carefully follow my every step, grabbing me if I slipped. The only problem was, my guardian angel would have gone down with me. It felt as though we were on an ice rink. Putting one foot carefully in front of the other, we advanced inch by inch on the slippery incline. With each step I could hear stones precipitated into the abyss, constantly reminding us of our danger. With my left hand I clung to whatever rock or branch I could, holding with my other hand onto the strings of the knapsack carried by the person in front of me — not so much as protection as to keep my direction. By holding onto that string, I was able to feel whether I needed to watch for an obstacle in front of me or whether a step up or down, to right or left, was required. When I felt the string tighten, I knew I could proceed in a straight line.

But all of a sudden, I felt the ground disappear beneath me. A piece of sodden earth had dislodged itself, making me lose my balance. I knew I was sliding down into the void, unable to catch myself this time. Withi seconds, Paul and the Nepalese men reacted. I felt muscular arms lifting me up. Everyone had to be extra careful, aware that the slightest wrong move might precipitate a further mudslide. All this didn't take more than a few seconds, but I remained frightened for a long time thereafter.

As soon as I felt myself on firm ground again, I started shaking all over, my legs no longer able to hold me up. It had started to rain again, I was soaked through, and my entire body was aching. But none of that mattered: we had survived.

By the end of the afternoon we arrived in Kathmandu, dirty, famished, and thoroughly exhausted.

Paul had risked his life with me on this dangerous journey. But why?

To have another stamp in his passport? For the school for the blind? Or . . .

'For you!' he exploded. 'Do you think I would have gone through all this for anyone else?'

'I see . . . ,' I said. I realized we were both letting off steam. 'So you took pity on me. You're convinced I wouldn't have been able to manage on my own!'

That sent Paul over the top. I had never known him to get so angry before. I confess it gave me a certain pleasure to push this always cheerful, always poised fellow to lose his temper.

'Stop the nonsense, Sabriye! It's about time you realized that you can't always do everything alone. And you are not alone in the world. For God's sake, there are people who really want to live and work with you. *Not* because they pity you. *Not* because they think you can't do it alone. But simply because they love you.'

He had said the word! Till now, I had only thought of him as a coworker, a dear friend in whom I could confide all my worries and thoughts. I had kept him at a distance, probably to protect myself from falling in love. Also, I was concerned love would jeopardize our friendship and the excellent work relationship we had created.

I had been fighting my feelings for him all along. Even tonight, I felt vulnerable and was still resisting his declaration of love to me. But finally, at the end of a long day, during which our lives had been saved at least three times, I gave in. We both understood the importance of the moment, and how precious and essential it was for us to face life, and all the problems inherent therein, not alone but together.

25

Two weeks later we received a fax. It was, alas, not the much-awaited reentry visas but a letter from my mother. And the news was alarming.

It seemed as if no one cared anymore about the fate of our blind children. Palden hadn't shown up at all since we had left, giving some vague sickness as a lame excuse. My mother had asked Chungda permission to take care of the children — a feat in itself, because ever since the Angello episode, access to the teaching unit was strictly forbidden to foreigners. As she went to our school, my mother discovered with dismay that there was no longer any classroom for our children. It had simply been shut down. All the children were in the kitchen, without any guidance, playing with their little blackboard and felt rounds. A Tibetan interpreter told my mother our kids missed us greatly and were lost without us, feeling abandoned; they never understood why we had left them. Faced with the school in such disarray, my mother didn't know which end was up, nor exactly what would happen to our children until we

271

returned. Who would do the teaching? She ran into Palden, who was apparently feeling better, and asked him to resume his teaching. After an embarrassed silence, Palden poured his heart out to Mother. He no longer wished to teach blind children. He found them stupid, and simply didn't feel up to the task anymore. All he wanted to do was teach 'normal' children from now on. And to top it off, Lopsang refused to let his orphans sit in the same classroom with blind pupils, because in his, Lopsang's, opinion, blind pupils were slower, and ultimately uneducable! Palden also revealed to my mother that the director had higher plans for him, anyway.

★　★　★

This news hit us both very hard and left us demoralized. Given this new development, was there any point in waiting here in Kathmandu for our reentry visas? It seemed clear now that our expulsion had been orchestrated to eliminate us and our project. Once we received our reentry visas, we would only go back long enough to pack our bags, close the school, and return the children to their respective families. After that, we would fly back to Europe, and that would be the end of our project.

Reality however, proved less dramatic. Thanks to my mother, who never let herself be defeated, and pestered Lopsang every day to help move things forward, we eventually did get our visas four days later, and we were off in a plane to Lhasa the next morning.

We arrived at the school, and to Paul's and my surprise, our children had been reintegrated into their old schoolroom. A much bigger surprise awaited us. Instead of Palden, my mother and Anila were both teaching the class! Hiding ourselves unnoticed behind the door, we observed the new scenario in utter disbelief.

'Nga gang la sum dom na gazo re?' (How much is five plus three?) my mother slowly articulated.

'Nga gang la sum, gya re!' (Five plus three equals eight!) the children replied in chorus.

We looked at each other in amazement. How had my mother — who didn't speak a word of Tibetan and didn't know the program — and Anila, the illiterate, arrived at this improbable and extraordinary point? And what was more, the children seemed neither sad nor disoriented; on the contrary, they were very attentive, clearly enjoying their lesson! The most astonishing aspect for us were the two remarkable ladies who had become teachers overnight. Here was my

273

mother, teaching math not only articulately but almost perfectly. As for Anila, she manipulated the felt rounds without making a single error, demonstrating braille characters to the children as if she had always taught braille. I had to remind myself that when she was first interviewed, we couldn't hire her as a teacher, merely as a supervisor. We were profoundly touched and impressed. What an astonishing transformation!

We stood there for a few minutes behind the classroom door, trying to make sense of this new development. Finally we made our entrance, and were greeted by loud hellos. The excited children jumped out of their seats and, in a chorus, broke into a German children's song my mother had taught them, followed by a Tibetan welcome song. This warm reception was followed by Norbu, who surprised us by reciting flawlessly the entire English alphabet in his high-pitched voice. Paul and I were overwhelmed. The past few days had not prepared us for this unexpected, and delightfully reassuring, scene.

After Palden's inglorious departure, my mother had pleaded with Lopsang to let her, Anila, and the children regain the use of their original classroom. Lopsang, probably tired of this relentless German woman who wouldn't give up, had relented and agreed. Ir the meantime, Mother and Anila furiously studied Tibetan braille for hours on end. They even went to the Banak Shol, asking some employees of the hotel to help them memorize a few mathematical formulas in Tibetan. Following my method, and with the help of the little *tsampa* balls I had devised, both women were able to teach our children to count, add, and subtract. Paul and I couldn't get over their courage, persistence, and downright gumption.

In similar circumstances anyone else would have thrown up their hands, defeated, and our children would have lost days and days of class instruction. But these two enterprising ladies, with their attitude of not taking no for an answer, had not only refused to admit defeat but performed a small miracle.

This said, we were terribly disappointed by Palden's conduct, he on whom we had counted so much. We couldn't fathom this abrupt change in him. Could he have been under relentless pressure from Lopsang? Whatever his reasons, we made up our minds not to let him get close to the children anymore and immediately started looking for another teacher.

My mother, it turned out, had already done the legwork for us.

'I believe I've found your teacher,' she

announced proudly. 'Her name is Nordon. She has just finished her studies, speaks excellent English, and what's more, would like to teach in the school for the blind!'

We owed Mother a mountain of gratitude for all sorts of things, but undoubtedly her greatest gift to us was Nordon. We met her and liked everything about her. She came from one of Lhasa's most noble families, was twenty-three, and according to Paul was very pretty and petite to the point of looking fragile. Paul and I wondered whether she would have enough stamina to withstand all the hardships this particular job entailed. Palden's example had demonstrated that one needed a special kind of perseverance to work with foreigners while staying on top of this unconventional job.

Our concerns turned out to be ill founded. Nordon proved not only to have great strength of character but above all an exceptional sense of mission, always anticipating with rare intuition any needs or problems our little blind ones might have. She made it eminently clear to us that her heart was in teaching.

Nordon started in right away, and within a few short days the children not only had forgotten Palden but had happily grown accustomed to their new teacher, who from the first day demonstrated special warm and cheerful ways of relating to each of them. She never took her eyes off them, it seemed, whether in class or out, and after taking time to study each one, she was able to devise teaching methods tailored to each particular need and personality.

In the case of Meto, who as mentioned still had a tiny fraction of vision left, Nordon drew on oversize sheets of paper large characters in bright colors, using the conventional Tibetan alphabet. As for Chila, whose hand coordination wasn't all it should have been, she tapped his imagination by calling on his talent for storytelling. To train his hands she made paper puppets that she slipped on each of Chila's fingers to illustrate his stories' characters. That forced him to concentrate on his hand movements, and using his fingers as actors helped him develop his hand coordination.

It had taken Nordon a mere few days to assimilate the Tibetan braille alphabet, and before we knew it she had prepared special notebooks for the children. Inspired by her, Norbu, Tendsin, and Meto were soon busy utilizing the braille typewriter with great dexterity. Already able to read much smaller characters than those learned previously, they were typing, each day at a faster pace, the short sentences Nordon was dictating to them. One day after class she came to see me.

'These little blind pupils are writing faster with their typewriter than sighted children do by hand!' she proudly announced.

The learning speed Meto, Tendsin, and Norbu displayed was such that we decided it would be a good idea to split the class into two groups. I would take care of the slower ones, Chila and Tashi, while Nordon would facilitate progress for the three others — who, obsessed with learning how to write, were always resentful when mealtime interrupted them, going so far to declare that all meals were an irritating intrusion on their program. Day in, day out, they couldn't wait for the morning prayer and breakfast to be over, after which they would run to their notebooks and typewriters. When evenings came, we couldn't tear them away from their desks — they were typing their homework for the next morning's class. We literally had to yank them off to bed each night. Obviously, turning the light off in their bedrooms was a meaningless act. Like so many children the world over, ours would simulate sleep, letting us peacefully bid them good night. As soon as we had left the dormitory, out came their braille notebooks from under the covers, and the reading would start. Even when they were ostensibly snoring, we could never be sure they weren't hiding a book in braille beneath the covers.

In a short time Norbu, Tendsin, and Meto had mastered writing entire sentences, as well as reading them perfectly out loud. Nordon tested them in their first exam, giving them dictation in Tibetan — not an easy assignment, particularly as the complex Tibetan spelling invites many mistakes with words that sounds alike but are spelled differently. So as not to make mistakes, they had to be diligent and learn to command each letter separately.

Chila, who had still not been able to learn to read or write fluently, could nonetheless spell correctly, thanks to his remarkable memory. As for Tashi, he had only mastered some twenty words; reading with his fingers on the braille board was still a challenge for him. Those two were given oral examinations, which Chila passed with flying colors, with Tashi trailing somewhat behind. Norbu and Meto were greatly excited at the idea of facing their first written exam, while Tendsin, glued to his desk and typewriter, chortled quietly, unmoved by his schoolmates' agitation.

'What could he be up to?' asked Nordon. 'He's so quiet it worries me. And what's all that chortling about?'

Suspecting something (and remembering my own school years), I moved over to where Tendsin was sitting. Running my hand under his desk, I was completely bowled over: he had placed his exercise book on his lap and was reading with one hand while writing with the other!

After reading all the exams, Nordon announced in a loud voice, 'Tendsin, one hundred!' Everyone congratulated him for his perfect mark. As for Tendsin, he was beaming. He also knew that no one suspected anything, other than me — and I had kept his little secret.

'Meto,' Nordon went on, 'ninety-seven!' She too was congratulated by one and all for her remarkable score. We all knew how hard she had recently worked to attain such a result. In fact, one evening she came to me and said, 'Could we please have one more teacher in our school? We have Sunday and three afternoons free. We want more lessons!'

'Norbu,' Nordon went on, 'eighty!' I had the feeling that this mediocre grade astonished him slightly. In the beginning, this naturally gifted child had been the best in the class, but Tendsin had not only caught up but passed him in math and writing. When he heard he had gotten only an 80, he threw himself on the ground and started to cry.

'I want to go home! I want to see my *amala!*'

'Why do you want to go back to your *amala?*' she asked.

'I'm homesick. And besides, I like *amala*'s cooking much better!' he said, starting to sob again. Taking him in her arms, Nordon soothed him, but the crying went on for quite some time, and nothing we could do seemed to console him.

'Any of you others want to return to your *amala?*' Nordon asked.

Meto shook her head, as did Tendsin.

'What would I do at home?' Tendsin said. 'I'm learning so much here. And having fun. That's the best gift I can make my *amala!*'

'Don't be sad, Anila is our real *amala*, anyway!' Tashi and Chila told Norbu.

In the middle of that night, as Paul was crossing the courtyard, still half asleep, on his way to use the school's bathroom — our own facilities had broken down months ago — he heard a noise. Probably a rat, he thought. But when the noise not only continued but grew louder, for a moment he feared it might be a burglar.

Tiptoeing toward the schoolroom, Paul leaned down and peeped through the keyhole. He saw a little figure seated at one of the class's desks. It was Norbu, who was whistling softly to himself, reading and writing, cheerfully oblivious to it being the middle of the night. He was no doubt preparing for his next exam — and this time, he had sworn to himself, he would get a 100!

Gyendsen, our sixth pupil, who had come to us through a German humanitarian agency at age eleven, taught us all that children have a rather unsentimental and pragmatic attitude about their blindness.

Gyendsen had become totally blind at the age of nine after suffering an eye infection that was not treated at the time. He had heard about our school but had no means to reach us, nor anyone to bring him — his village being far away and cut off from the rest of the country during the rainy season. Extremely intelligent and dynamic, he was not only an excellent horseman but also a good swimmer. He had already attended school previous to coming to us. Learning braille was no problem for him, and within a short time he had caught up with Norbu, Tendsin, and Meto.

Anila and I had become Nordon's teaching aides. The three of us had together devised a good program that consisted of teaching reading, writing, mathematics, and Chinese. When we handed out the new curriculum schedule, Gyendsen suggested we add

English to the program.

'If we learn English,' he said, 'we'll finally be able to talk to Gen Polo.'

'Gen Polo' was the name they had given Paul, who was still wrestling with only a few phrases in Tibetan, and had become the constant butt of their jokes. So we did add English to our curriculum, and soon saw that this radically improved communications between them. We had all forgotten how fast children can absorb new languages, and Tendsin and Gyendsen in particular learned English amazingly fast. In no time flat, both were conversing in simple but fully constructed sentences.

Judging by the permanent smile on his face, it was clear to all of us that Gyendsen was enjoying school. One day Nordon asked him to tell everyone what he saw when he could still see, and explain what happened when he became blind. The thing he most remembered, Gyendsen explained, were his eyes. His eye infection had given him great pain.

'When my eyes stopped hurting, though, things were fine again.' Then he told us this significant anecdote. 'One day, after I had gone blind, I was on the back of a truck, driving along the edge of a cliff. The other passengers were all getting seasick as they looked down the precipice. But since I couldn't see the danger, I remained calm and happy. That was my personal advantage over them all!' At which point his little audience broke into a laughter of approval.

About the same time Gyendsen arrived at our school, Chungda came to deliver a message from her father: we should stop taking in blind students. In fact, he no longer wanted to have us as colleagues. We were to vacate the premises by year's end.

Once again our project was in mortal danger. We were too vulnerable. I would have to find a way to change our precarious situation. I had no idea where we might relocate and was terribly upset. Paul and I repaired to the garden to talk things over quietly.

Nordon, who had followed us, did her best to console us and stiffen our spines.

'You can't give up your school now! You have a fine reputation in Lhasa, and the blind children are not only learning well but are extremely happy here! You can't just drop them!'

'But Nordon, what do you expect us to do when we find ourselves out in the gutter this winter?'

'Buy a house. That way you won't be dependent on anyone!'

'Great idea,' Paul said wryly. 'But how in the world can we buy a house when we don't even have enough money to run the school?'

Since our return from Nepal, we had been operating on a shoestring. Our organization back home was playing its usual game of not transferring money on time, making us sweat. Our personal resources were drying out, and once again we were faced with the imminent prospect of not being able to feed our children or pay our staff. Both Anila and Nordon had agreed to temporarily forgo their salaries, and some humanitarian organizations in Lhasa offered to advance us some money in case of dire need.

I sent a long letter to Germany, enclosing a detailed report of the extraordinary results of our teaching, the blossoming of the children, and our future plans, i.e. the creation of a much-needed rehabilitation center and vocational school. I also described the critical financial situation we were in, imploring them to give us wider room to expand. Last but not least, I asked to be allowed to make key decisions that would improve the running of the school.

A few weeks later their answer reached me:

Dear Sabriye,

We are aware that, thanks to you and your dedication, you gave birth to this project. But our organization must, however, retain the right to make all executive decisions regarding the further development of the project.

You will be a delegate of our organization, and as such you will not dispose of the same freedom of action you had while putting the project together. I understand this new situation may not please you. Rest assured that this is not our decision. We are obliged to impose this mode of conduct if we are to be further involved in the development of your project . . .

Important decisions, such as the prolongation of the project, moving to another building, or any change of a Tibetan partnership will be dictated and approved only by us, and are henceforth no longer your responsibility.

We will of course listen to your suggestions, but will ultimately remain the ones to decide. Should your project fail, the ministry will not hold you responsible. Our organization, and its board of directors, will take full responsibility. As for any report on school's activities, it is henceforth for us to establish the rules.

I am certain that you are giving your best efforts to the project at Lhasa, and I am not unaware of all the difficulties you have had to surmount. Don't think for a moment it's easy for me to take over the responsibility and start giving you orders — especially you, the woman who has created our Tibetan structure. We both have the same objective, and I hope that, with time, we will both fulfill our respective roles better.

End of letter. That was all. No mention of any transfer of money whatsoever. I later learned that the organization never even sent my report on to the ministry but created another one — one that served their own purposes better. As a result, the secretary at the ministry who had been sponsoring me until now began to lose confidence in my ability to bring the project to fruition.

In the fall of 1998 I decided to return to Germany and see for myself what was going on both at the association and at the ministry. Paul too had to go back to Europe, so we decided to close the school and announced a three-week vacation. The children would all go back home. Everyone was delighted. With their books under their arms, they were already making plans to regale their families and friends all about our school, about braille, and about what they had learned and done in Lhasa.

26

Many projects begun in foreign countries have the good fortune to benefit from government grants. Unfortunately, as in my case, the Ministry of Education, or any other official government department, several thousand miles from where the project was put together, may reserve the right to make all decisions concerning the establishment and running of the project. People working locally on the project are too often deprived of the right to make decisions on the spot. How wrongheaded that is! From so far away, how can this system be efficient?

The hierarchy is simple: At the top, the official organism responsible for financing, such as the Federal Ministry for Economic Cooperation and Aid to Development, selects which projects merit its attention and funding. For a smaller project, the same ministry appoints another organization, which will act as a sponsor under the ministry's supervision. Even smaller projects, those at the bottom of the ladder, in need of a financial subsidy, must seek out such an organization. It was made clear to me that those who originate a project and develop it are but mere employees of the system, and have to respect the rules.

In many instances, this authoritarian structure has a destructive, even devastating, effect on the project.

Those like ourselves who run a project and function within it in foreign lands — as active participants who speak the language, know the local habits and rules, and are ultimately familiar with the goings-on of the country and the project — are infinitely better placed to make appropriate decisions than bureaucrats sitting thousands of miles away. Only those who've worked all along on a project can evaluate it correctly. Together with the higher officials responsible for the endowment — who sit on the other side of the world — they can move any given project forward. That's how it should ideally be. Sadly, this was not my case.

I should have picked another organization to sponsor me. But of course that's hindsight — and, I reminded myself, I didn't know other organizations back then. I imagined that their role consisted in reading and assessing my reports, signing some letters, and mostly acting as a conduit between the ministry and me, processing our money transfers regularly. How naive I was.

What I had no reason to know at the time, and only discovered later in the game, was that my sponsoring organization proved incompetent in processing the simplest forms, and incapable of addressing any of the details commensurate with such partnership. For a start, its president had no clue where Tibet was on the map — as I found out later — nor where it stood politically. Could her inability to locate Tibet on the map explain the enormous delays in my money transfers?

★ ★ ★

A week or so after I was back in Germany, a friend read me the report written by the president of the organization to the ministry. I couldn't believe my ears, and the more I heard, the angrier I became. The report covered everything except our mission, our educational concept, our activities, and how our project had evolved over these past several months and would in the future. Instead, the association's president went into lengthy detail about my conflicts with Lopsang, from a very subjective point of view — the president's evaluation was based on her three-day trip to Lhasa the previous August, following her extended stay in China proper. That the furniture and other materials 'purchased for our school' by the director, for which money had been transferred by the organization, had been logged in the ledger but never bought was, according to her, pure slander on my part! The report claimed that the director and his daughter had produced ample documentation and receipts for the president, demonstrating that sums of money had been transferred to the school for the blind but never spent by them, by implication pointing the guilty finger at me. The orphan institute, it went on, had in fact loaned us money. And as for the furniture, it was all stored in their warehouse, waiting to be delivered. That the president had never bothered to go to the warehouse to verify this, or that I had personally been obliged to take $10,000 from my own savings and put it into the school, was not mentioned. Nor did she bother to point out that the children had been sleeping on bedsprings, waiting in vain for the director to deliver mattresses.

The report went on to accuse me of lacking in teaching background and experience, as a result of which I did not have the professional equipment required to carry on this project. Furthermore, the children, according to her report, were not receiving an adequate education. 'The teaching,' it said, 'is both irregular and without adequate planning.'

I was aghast. How could I explain such an incredible distortion of facts, such lies? The president, from those many thousand miles away, must have felt left out, and needed to present an image of herself in control of the situation to the ministry.

Once again, I was appalled at my naïveté! Here I was, for the first time in my life, the object of slander, and I never even saw it coming! This was entirely foreign and new to me — my first lesson in basic human behavior. I was growing up fast. Only a year ago the functionaries at the ministry had paid close attention when I outlined my plans and projects, and now they wouldn't even listen to my side of the story.

Officials at the ministry told me over the phone in no uncertain terms, 'You're no longer the person we will be communicating with regarding the Tibetan project. Any issue or problems will have to be addressed to us through your organization.' Nonetheless, the ministry agreed to let me take part in a forthcoming meeting between the president of the organization and the ministry. I couldn't wait for the promised meeting, but it occurred to me that if only I could meet with the members of the association before the big get-together at the ministry, things could perhaps be ironed out. A face-to-face could only be helpful, for I needed to know why all my letters and faxes had gone unanswered.

The president had personally composed the report to the ministry — written, she said proudly, only the night before the deadline. I wasn't surprised; it certainly read that way. I prepared a detailed memo pointing out all the factual errors in this report, which I handed to the vice president at the start of the meeting. The vice president read it, then handed it to the president, who hardly glanced at it, then declared, 'I was hoping we might have a friendly meeting. However, under the circumstances . . . '

The other board members at the table remained painfully silent, doubtless understanding that by signing off on her report, they had put me in an untenable situation. The vice president and the treasurer, doubtless to justify what they had done, said that since the president's report had been prepared at the last minute, they really had not had time to read it over as carefully as they should have.

Taking advantage of this interruption, I presented a quick résumé of our activities and several successes in Tibet. I went on for a good ten minutes, and I saw that I had their attention. But when I had finished, not a question, not a comment, not a word of advice or encouragement. Then the president responded maliciously: 'My dear Sabriye, I can see how well you have mastered the art of presentation. Knowing how to convince an audience is a precious asset. We should hire you to help us get more money from our sponsors.'

'If I understand you correctly, you don't believe me,' I said.

'I do realize,' the president answered, 'that some progress has been made in Tibet since you arrived.'

'If you had paid any attention to my letters, you would have learned that much earlier.'

'Your letters!' she cried out, her voice dripping with disdain. 'Without exception, they were begging for money, outlining your unrealistic projects for a vocational school and all sorts of other impractical ideas. More recently, you went so far as to ask for funds to buy a house! Really, Sabriye!'

'It's high time you responded to my urgent appeals, instead of never responding. Without funds, the project is dead. In less than two months we'll be on the street, children, teachers, everybody. It's imperative we come up with a solution!'

All of a sudden the president seemed less sure of herself. To judge from the remarks made around the table, it was clear that my correspondence had never been shared with the board members.

The treasurer stood up.

'I'm afraid we've been largely kept in the dark about your project. What can we do at this stage?'

'If you granted me the right to make necessary decisions, and — '

'It does seem to me that it makes perfect sense for Sabriye to be the one making informed decisions on the spot!' the treasurer persisted courageously.

The president cut him off. 'Any decision regarding the Tibetan school is our organization's sole responsibility!' Then she said, 'Now, let's look at the contract.'

I had been waiting for this famous document for over six months. I had never understood why it hadn't been sent.

Hearing it for the first time, I was astounded by its contents. If I understood correctly, the only thing I would be allowed to do would be to teach braille in Tibetan. I was stripped of all other power and responsibility. All the furniture and teaching material henceforth belonged exclusively to the organization. And as a final blow, my salary would be cut in half, from this day on.

'What does all this mean?' I asked angrily. 'Am I to consider this a form of punishment?

And for what, may I ask?'

After a long silence, I heard the treasurer's hesitant voice: 'As a matter of fact, we discussed this at great length with the board of directors. In your original proposal, you spoke of ten children, and you still have only six.'

'Right, my original figure had been ten. Finding children throughout the country, often hidden in the dark by their families in faraway villages, has proved a slow and tricky process. Are you telling me I'm paid by the student? You've remained deaf to all my requests and reports, you've never participated in any of the planning and structure. I work under the most trying circumstances. I must remind you that my salary, such as it is, was agreed upon from the start. Not to mention that it is not *your* money but that of public funding!'

'You don't really believe we'll send you the same salary to teach ten children when in reality you're only teaching six?' the president said icily.

We were going around in circles, getting nowhere. Suddenly, the vice president remembered he had an important meeting. So did the president. So much for my hope of clarifying the situation. The meeting was adjourned.

Waking up the day of the ministry meeting, I burst into tears for the first time since I was a little girl. The magnitude of the injustice overwhelmed me. How would I ever be able to fight the incredible slanders, the lies stacked against me by powerful bureaucrats? I felt defeated before I started.

The previous night I had been so upset I took refuge at my parents'. Worried to see me so upset, they offered me a big cup of mint tea and some oatmeal in an effort to calm me down. It seemed to do the trick. After I had regained better control of myself, my parents and I started strategizing.

The plan was for me to arrive a good half hour before the meeting with my documents — several copies of them — and pictures of each child, of the class in progress, of the school, and of Tibet in general. The idea was for me to engage in casual conversation with those arriving for the meeting, hoping that looking at the pictures and listening to me might perhaps pique their curiosity, perhaps even soften them and dispose some of them to be in my favor before the meeting.

Armed with this little plan, I arrived at the ministry a good twenty minutes early. A woman whose job it was to accompany me upstairs, turned up a couple minutes after I arrived. I introduced myself, and she replied curtly, 'I know who you are. Please follow me.'

I'm used to people taking my arm, or at least offering to guide me. This woman simply walked off leaving me to fend for myself. I wasn't sure she had been told I was blind. I managed to get through a revolving door, but trying to keep up with her made me bang my head quite loudly against the half-open elevator door.

'Dear me,' she said, 'I'm not used to taking care of blind people!'

As I followed her through the labyrinth of corridors, I was determined to carry out my plan. I tried engaging her in some kind of conversation about Tibet, despite the growing bump on my forehead, that was beginning to hurt. I quickly gave up. Finally we arrived at the conference room, where my guide offered to seat me anywhere I liked. 'But you should know,' she said, 'it's unlikely any of the participants will be here for a good hour.' Aha, I thought, so I'm not considered a participant, I see. A few minutes later, the head of some department walked over to me.

'Ms. Tenberken,' he said, taking a seat next to me, 'we have every intention of examining any solution you might propose. But I must beg you to please abstain, if you possibly can, from blaming our organization for your problems. That would put us in a catastrophic situation.'

I agreed I would measure my words.

While we were waiting for the others to show up, our moderator informed us that several members of the commission were caught in traffic jams. I suggested that we show the little video of our school that I had brought with me. That didn't go over particularly well; they expressed no interest in seeing the video. So much for that little plan. So I suggested showing them pictures of the children. The lack of interest was even greater.

Before long, the representatives of the organization trickled in one by one, followed by the members of the commission. Aware that the first item on their agenda was to address the president's report, I nevertheless pleaded to begin the meeting with a presentation of our project.

'The commission from the ministry has no interest in viewing the school for the blind from the perspective of an employee of the organization,' the ministry moderator informed me. 'You should be grateful we invited you to this meeting. The president's report has been read and approved, and the commission has found it satisfactory.' The other members agreed with him, with the exception of the man who had first entered — the head of some department, whose name I never knew.

I understood that from that point on the meeting would be a charade. It was clear that everything had been prearranged and gone over in detail long before by the president. They merely tolerated my presence, and no one had the slightest intention of letting me change their minds, which were clearly made up. I should have left the meeting on the spot.

The association president got up and made her presentation to the assembled members, talking about her organization mainly, justifying every step taken by it, along the way, giving almost no time to the School for the Blind in Tibet. Nor was there any mention of the fact that the school was about to be obliterated, thrown into the street.

I jumped up and, apologizing for the interruption, blurted out, 'For several months we've been aware that the situation of our school was extremely precarious. We've been asked to vacate the space before the end of the year.'

The department head seemed completely aken aback. 'This is a terribly serious

301

problem,' he said, 'of which none of us was aware.'

'Unfortunately, we've had plenty of time to be aware of it in Lhasa, I assure you. And I believe I have found the solution.'

'It sounds to me that the simplest and most logical thing would be to put Sabriye Tenberken in charge,' said the department head.

The president immediately expressed her disagreement, reiterating in no uncertain terms it was the organization's job, not mine.

'She's right! We have to be careful this doesn't turn into a Tenberken project!' echoed the bureaucrat I had first met. And a chorus of murmured approval was heard around the table.

So that part of the meeting was over.

Next on the agenda was our budget. Only half of our subsidy had been sent to Tibet, the department head noted.

'Ladies and gentlemen,' I chimed in, 'since last September we've been working under terrific financial constraints. When we didn't receive any of the funds due us from you, I had to take money from my private savings account to tide us over. That was not in the plan, and it cannot continue.'

'Sabriye, your school seems to have had so many problems since its inception that we made the decision not to forward any further funds to you until problems were solved.'

Why did no one question her position? Point out that her failure to forward government funds was gross negligence? Didn't they understand that our children and staff were the victims of some unrelated power struggle?

I had had about enough of this charade. Fortunately, the meeting was adjourned. As I left the building, I made a resolution: if nothing changed in our favor — and I couldn't imagine at this juncture what would — I decided right then and there to go it alone with Paul, Nordon, and Anila, with the help of some private subsidy, which I felt sure I could raise one way or another. In any case, I wanted out with these bureaucrats. Forever.

★　★　★

Three months later, Paul and I took the final step of going it on our own, and we realized that the decision was the best we could have made.

We are currently able to bring our project to fruition without any interference or roadblock from either a distant, clueless organization or a misinformed governmental department. Separating ourselves from official government support was a big relief. Though our life has been fraught with problems, we have never for a moment regretted our decision. Had we not taken that critical step that winter, our Project for the Blind, Tibet would have died a pitiful death.

27

As luck would have it, that year we experienced our first long, harsh, pitiless Tibetan winter. Throughout that season, the temperature never went above freezing. Whatever the Tibetans claim — and they do maintain that the Lhasa Valley climate is always pleasant — toes start to freeze in November, and thaw out only in March. No heating system exists anywhere in the country, not even electric heaters: they would provoke electrical blackouts in entire neighborhoods! The more modern buildings, built by the southern Chinese, were not conceived for the harsh Tibetan winters. Lack of insulation in the concrete walls results in temperatures as freezing inside as out, where a glacial wind sweeps permanently and mercilessly.

Each day began with the same ritual: Paul would scrape thick coats of ice off our windows. Our water basin was always covered with a lid of ice, and I understood for the first time why Tibetans don't like to wash between mid-September and the end of March. I confess I've often dreamed of adopting that habit as well.

Each fall, in preparation for the cold months to come, men and women go off on a collective picnic by a shallow river. There, the festivities start: all of them immerse themselves in the river and thoroughly wash and shampoo themselves. Throughout the winter that follows, body upkeep is limited to smearing yak butter all over the body — a preservative against frostbite — as well as into the hair, which prevents it from breaking off.

Having been reared in the West with its excessive focus on hygiene, I still find it difficult to get used to these practices — even though, in this Tibetan climate, they seem practical in so many ways. Defying Tibetan principles, I paid a bitter price for my obsession with hygiene. One day, after washing my hair in the evening, I woke up the next morning with stiff, iced hair like stalactites, frozen against my pillow. Paul had to come to my rescue and yank the pillow off my hair.

But the harsh winter conditions seemed to affect only us. Paul and I couldn't get over how cheerful the children were in the face of the horrendous cold. It all seemed normal to them. They read and wrote in our freezing classroom, wearing only wool caps and heavy lined jackets. I couldn't understand how their little hands could remain warm. In the main, good health prevailed, with the exception of one child whose cold both Paul and I caught — mine evolving into a nasty bronchitis, and Paul's into pneumonia. Aware that Tibet lacks adequate medication, I kept a vigilant eye on Paul.

December 25 was the coldest day we had ever experienced. During the night, all the water pipes froze, and our courtyard turned into an ice-skating rink. I could only cross it by sitting on my rear end. Of course, sliding on the ice became a source of great entertainment for all the children.

Anila was busy making breakfast in our warm kitchen, behind big pots of hot tea, and for the first time I too downed my hot buttered tea with newfound pleasure. It would doubtless cure my bronchitis. As for Paul, he was still sick in bed and couldn't shake his fever. The preparations for the Christmas celebrations were left up to Anila, Nordon, our new cook, Yishi, and me.

At the beginning of our stay in Tibet, Paul and I were certain that Western Christmas was ignored in this part of the world. That turned out not to be the case. Nordon had taught the children to sing, 'We wish you a merry Christmas and a Happy New Year,' which they sang to me at the slightest provocation. She had also told them all about our Christmas traditions, and they were eager to share them with us. While Yishi and Anila were busy baking biscuits and various cakes, Nordon and I went off to the tailor to pick up some clothes we had ordered for the children. To reach his shop at the end of the old town, one had to first climb a set of slippery stairs that had been smeared with yak butter, then walk through corridors from whose ceiling hung large slices of dried meat. In his studio, jam-packed to the ceiling with piles of wool, cotton, *tsubas* (silk, wool, and brocade coats), monks' pants, and robes, the tailor was seated behind a wooden table. He smiled as he watched us make our way awkwardly through the mounds of clothes. He proudly showed us the jackets we had ordered, which were made of red fabric with gold braids and lined with soft fur. He had also made some dark blue pants, also decorated with gold braids. Knowing these outfits were intended for blind children, he had ingeniously sewn on the pockets and decorated the pants the same way inside and out — that way, he figured, if they put their pants on inside out, they'd still be fine. We were touched by his thoughtfulness. With my fingers, I felt how luxurious these new clothes were.

When our children received their new

outfits — veritable works of art — they squealed, fully understanding how beautiful the gifts were. Chila turned to Tashi and with a serious expression told him, 'You better be careful never to dirty those new pants, or else!'

More shopping needed to be done for our big Christmas dinner — some china bowls, candles, and new chopsticks, and a few other things — and Nordon and I went back into town.

There were always several young men hanging around us like tomcats, trying to catch Nordon's attention. But she ignored them, telling them that her work with the blind children was her first priority. One persistent suitor, however, who didn't take no far an answer and who she couldn't shake, managed to accompany us all the way to town. He had less chance than any of the others, Nordon explained to me; her mother wouldn't look too kindly on her going out with a Chinese man.

We returned to find our 'living room' already filled with guests. Dolma, her husband, and their children had arrived and were playing with the fountain's icicles; Norbu, Yishi's two teenage children, a friend of Anila with her five-year-old daughter, and another friend were already there as well. Of the eighteen, I was the only Westerner: seventeen Tibetans, and one Chinese, Nordon's suitor.

Dolma, Nordon, and I had had great fun decorating the tables back to back to form a long table. We had placed candles all along its center, with bowls of treats. In the middle of the room, a Christmas tree offered by my parents stood proudly.

By six that evening, everyone was called in. I heard their long sigh of admiration. Our usual classroom had been turned into a festive place. Delicious aromas permeated the air, and Anila and Yishi were ready to serve us what promised to be a real feast.

Each of our guests had contributed to it by bringing gifts of all sorts: baskets of strawberries from southern China, other baskets filled to the rim with oranges and bananas, trays of *khabse* (little fritters with sugar, cooked in yak butter), still crisp and warm, trays of sliced pork and yak meat, pickles, and a huge container of cold, spicy tomato soup and traditional *momos*, the meatballs made of yak meat and cooked in a broth. There was also plenty of sweet tea with milk and Coca-Cola handy.

Before sitting down, each child was given a red balloon and asked to blow it up and bounce it skyward, which they did with screams of joy. Then the entire group, adults and children alike, broke into European Christmas songs, accompanied by rhythmic clapping. Even Tashi, who normally could not remember any song in class, seemed transformed and was singing away, at the top of his lungs, English, Chinese, and traditional Tibetan songs.

Our Christmas party was a total success, the children overwhelmed by the generous buffet. Having never been exposed to so much food at one time, they were helping themselves with gusto to the various treats on display. The focus on eating was such, in fact, that all chitchat subsided, with only sounds of chewing and groans of appreciation.

'Go ahead, serve yourself, Gyendsen! Today is *chrisse misse*, you can take as much as you want!' Chila encouraged the shy boy.

As the evening was winding down, everyone grabbed the phone as I called Germany to wish my parents Merry Christmas. The thought of my parents being involved in our celebration pleased me greatly. As I was about to retire to my apartment, I was once again touched by my colleagues, who surrounded me, handing me their home-made Christmas presents: lovely cards they had each hand-painted.

The end of a perfect day.

28

Shortly after Christmas, we started packing, preparing to leave. Though he was still down with pneumonia, Paul insisted on dragging himself out of bed and, much against our will, helped us pack.

Fortunately, a humanitarian organization had volunteered a van, as well as a few men, to help us move. Also, one of Lhasa's shopkeepers had offered to lend us some crates and big canvas bags to pack our things into. After much effort on everyone's part, we were finally set for our big move.

'Where are you going?' Chungda inquired as she came to watch us wrap our dishes.

'To the street, of course. We're bound to find a good corner on the Beijing Dong Lu for the children and all our things, don't you think?' Paul let out.

As the moment for our departure approached, Lopsang, Chungda, and their entourage made themselves scarce. In fact, we never saw them again. The orphanage staff were the only ones offering us a hand, and some *katags* as good-bye gifts. The orphans longtime playmates of our blind children

312

couldn't understand why we were leaving. They were the only ones to see us off, crowded on the balcony and waving sadly as we drove away.

A page of our adventure had just turned.

Our biggest, most extraordinary Christmas present had come from Nordon's mother, who had offered us the hospitality of her big house until we found permanent quarters. Nordon's family lived in a wonderful Tibetan-style compound, built in the 1950s. In size and layout, it seemed perfect for our needs — as if it had been conceived with us in mind.

The gate opened onto a courtyard — again, perfect for our children to play ball or other games. The main house had been built over a big basement — a rarity in Tibet. We had to climb up a few steps to enter the house with its four large rooms, each with big windows, and a small kitchen. Around the house there was also a barn and several stables. A big garden spread behind, with two big old weeping willows that the children soon learned to climb.

The whole setup struck us as both serene and bucolic; a puppy, attached to his wooden little kennel, and a few chickens pecking on a and pile added to the entrancing scene.

Nordon's mother, Amala, standing in the

middle of the courtyard, was waiting impatiently to welcome us. She was open, warm, lively; we all liked her instantly. Despite her limited knowledge of English, we got along fine. Obviously cultivated, she spoke excellent Chinese, and a smattering of Russian.

'Welcome! I love your country! You Germans have the best beer, and of course Karl Marx!'

It was clear she enjoyed the good things in life. In any case, she immediately took to our little blind children. She was delighted to have them, she said. Nordon told us that her mother was impatient for her daughters to marry and bring home some grandchildren. That remark had inspired Nordon to suggest she take us in, which she graciously did.

We started unpacking, but Amala interrupted us with 'Shu den dscha' (Please come in!), inviting us inside before we unpacked to enjoy some refreshments. Everything was ready for our welcome in the dining room. We sat on benches along the windows, covered with thick, beautiful rugs, and were invited to help ourselves at the large table laden with cakes and fruit. Probably worn out by our moving day, the children were rather quiet and unusually shy, helping themselves only modestly to the generous offerings. But the all awoke from their lethargy when Nordon turned on the television set in one corner of the room. Never having been exposed to television, they were completely startled and awed. Who were the people in that machine? they all asked. Meto, with her minuscule bit of eyesight, pressed her face against the screen, which she mistook for a window. Whatever she could vaguely perceive was moving so fast she lost patience. Norbu for his part had stumbled on a mike, and was calling everyone to quickly come and feel the mike fixed on a base. As soon as they located the switch and turned it on, their fatigue magically vanished and they all began singing, mike in hand.

Luckily, Amala was able to stop this unwelcome concert by luring them back to the table.

For the next several hours we went about unpacking. Crates and bags were emptied; others were stacked temporarily in the house and the courtyard. A few hours later, after we had finished arranging the children's belongings as neatly as possible, Amala invited us all back in for a welcome dinner — which turned out to be an extraordinary feast.

As night fell, Gyendsen, Tendsin, and Meto were pressed into service to help us roll out our sleeping bags in one of the big empty rooms; Chila and Tashi were taking advantage of the last rays of sun, sitting on a stone outside, telling each other stories. As for Norbu, he was having a wild time, mercilessly chasing the resident sheep and dog, as well as the chickens, around the courtyard. The resident rooster, however, not at all appreciating the fun, stood in an attack position, ready to scratch this insolent intruder. Suddenly afraid, Norbu ran behind a tree and straight into Nordon's mother's arms. 'Ama! Ama!' he called to her.

We would have much preferred getting settled in with the children at Nordon's home. But foreigners, we knew, were not allowed to stay in private Tibetan homes, so Paul and I moved back into Banak Shol.

In no time at all Amala became the children's friend, adoptive mother, and teacher. On Sundays and during rest periods, she would come and teach them diction, songs, and the art of Tibetan dance. She often invited friends for informal little performances, at which the children sang their latest songs. If our children expressed some nervousness, she would reassure them, infusing them with self-confidence.

'It's very important for you to show the world what you can do!' she insisted. 'You *can* sing and dance, you *can* read and write, and be just as happy as all the other children. No one is allowed to keep you from having fun. No one can ever again lock you up. Never be afraid of anything, or ashamed of who you are!' I was pleased that this newcomer corroborated everything we had been teaching the children all along. They listened intently to what she had to say, and it had its effect. One day, as we were taking a walk along the Barkhor, some nomads made derogatory remarks about Chila and Gyendsen, calling them 'dumb blind kids.' Chila started to cry.

'You must learn to defend yourself,' said Amala, drying his tears. 'No one is allowed to destroy your self-confidence. No one.'

Gyendsen had learned his lesson well. In a loud voice that made passersby turn their heads, he shouted to the nomads, 'You have no right to speak about us like that! We're blind, yes, but not dumb. And what about you? I bet you can't even read or write, can you? You've never gone to school, have you? And I know you're incapable of finding toilets at night without any light?'

This simple reaction confirmed that our efforts had not been in vain.

★ ★ ★

The Tibetan New Year, called Losar, is usually celebrated between the end of January and the beginning of March. The date is different each year, and varies from district to district, even from village to village.

In Lhasa, the celebrations for Losar began on the twenty-ninth day of the last Tibetan calendar month. Tradition calls for families to sit down together before dusk, and *guthuk* — a special soup with noodles and nine specific ingredients, which symbolize peace, joy of having children, wealth, and happiness — is served in two tureens. Everyone eats his or her soup, making sure the first tureen is emptied. The contents of the second tureen are then tossed out ceremoniously into the street to ensure that the previous year's demons are chased away.

As night fell on this New Year, all of Lhasa seemed to take to the streets, armed with firecrackers, which they set off every second, it seemed, on every corner. Fierce firecracker battles were waged throughout the city, and Lhasa's streets were enveloped in smoke and the pungent smell of sulfur. The idea was for each street to try and produce the loudest noise, drowning out that of the next street — again, in an effort to chase demons away.

The noise managed to scare Paul and me more than it did the demons, I'm certain

Clinging to each other in our room at the Banak Shol, we wondered if we were really safe and prayed for this insane celebration to end.

With its thin partitions, our ten-by-ten hotel room was barely big enough for a bed, desk, and washbasin. It had the advantage of being near our temporary school at Amala's, and was relatively inexpensive. We sat on the bed listening to the wild concert, or rather cacophony, trying to reflect on all that had happened to our school and us in these past few months. To exorcise our own demons, I decided to write the organization that had failed to sponsor us, or at least help us financially, the following letter of resignation:

Ever since my first year at the university, I nurtured the dream of putting a project together in Tibet. And that dream has now become a reality. To arrive at the stage we have reached, however, I have had to invest all my resources, energy, and personal savings.

Each day has brought me the infinite reward of seeing our children blossom, from the time we first found them abandoned and wasting away, shy and depressed, until today, when all of them are eager to learn and for the first time are smiling and happy. This undertaking has inspired and energized me every step of the way. But you are not unaware that our work in Tibet has been fraught with daily, sometimes insurmountable bureaucratic obstacles, both in Tibet and in Germany.

All of us at the school have dedicated ourselves to the project seven days a week and thought nothing of putting in a fourteen-hour day, without so much as a weekend break or any vacation — a fact that would have been deemed objectionable and unacceptable in any Western country.

Our living conditions have also been near impossible in a country where any type of heating in houses is unknown, medical welfare vastly insufficient, and last but not least, where bureaucracy and its red tape have to be the worst in the world. Nonetheless, we have never complained. In such harsh circumstances and difficult living conditions, an occasional word of encouragement from the sponsoring organization would have been more than welcome. A letter from you back in Europe, in your comfortable offices, offering positive criticism, perhaps even spiced now and again with some sort of praise, however faint, would have made all the difference . . .

Despite your personal silence, and that of your board of directors, and your manifest indifference to our plight and problems, I refrained from voicing my disappointment and frustration.

Still, I am puzzled as to why, after taking my project on as sponsors, you have chosen never to answer any of my numerous requests for assistance or counsel. I am equally curious about why, time and time again, you failed to transfer monies due the project as per our original agreement. I also gravely question why our generous investors were never given copies of my reports, which provided them with a progress report of our school.

All the above makes me seriously question both your position and our future relationship.

I can only impute these failings to the fact that, being so far away, your organization must have been over-whelmed, the task at hand clearly beyond the capabilities of your staff. Our project is solidly up and running and, thanks to our unstinting personal efforts to date, has given courage and a new faith in the future to six bright children, with many more to follow.

I believe the time has therefore come for me to pursue this mission on my own. You may take this letter as my formal request to end our collaboration. I sincerely hope this separation will leave us on the best of terms.

Sincerely yours,
Sabriye

After the letter was mailed, Paul and I felt immensely relieved.

★ ★ ★

Thus began the Year of the Hare and the Earth for us — with neither funding, nor a roof over our heads, and without the least knowledge of what our future would be. We braced ourselves, aware that this transition period — before we found new financing — would be extremely difficult. We knew we had traded temporary loss of financial support for freedom and independence, but the trade-off had given us new strength to go forward.

One day, shortly after classes had begun in our temporary quarters, Amala took Paul and me aside: 'How would you feel about buying the house you're in, including its garden and surrounding outbuildings?'

Dumbfounded, we couldn't find any words to respond.

'Listen to me carefully,' she said. 'This house has become too big for me and the children. I know financing is a concern to you. Please don't worry about it. I can wait a few years. I know you are seeking new investors, and I urge you to focus on your school, your children, and their welfare. I also know that your school for the blind will do our family name proud!'

A gift from heaven! We felt Amala's offer was solid and straight from the heart. How could we not accept?

29

That unexpected and extraordinarily generous offer opened all kinds of new possibilities for us, lifted our spirits, and infused us with renewed strength. As soon as we signed the contract with Amala, Paul and I threw ourselves into a frenzy of renovation. A new life was about to begin for our school.

Together we were able to install the children's dormitory. We transformed the stables into classrooms. It was a great deal of work, but our motivation saw us through.

With the help of a few workers Paul had hired, we built and installed a good working kitchen for Yishi, with a brand-new stove. Paul installed a new drainage system as well. But when Paul built two toilets — one Tibetan style, the other European — the entire neighborhood, who had never seen our kind of toilet, came to pay its respects, exclaiming, 'Ozi-ah!'

Our European-style facility was the envy of everyone, so much so in fact we had to lock it to keep the whole neighborhood from using it. Another bonus of being in Amala's house: we enjoyed Nordon's highly respected family's protection. For the first time in a long while, we worked with the continual endorsement and approval of the community, a feeling we appreciated all the more after the painful, distrustful months spent with Lopsang and Chungda.

One day we received what seemed to us an outrageously high electrical bill. Amala was furious and showed it to all our neighbors. Like wildfire, the information spread from house to house, and the next thing I knew, all the neighbors — a dozen or so — marched off to the electrical company, my bill in hand.

Initially ignored by the local bureaucrats, our group refused to leave.

'But these are foreigners, can't you see?' the electrical employee told our stolid group. 'They have enough money for us to charge them twenty times the normal cost if we decide to!'

'These foreigners are not what you think,' one of our neighbors said. 'They happen to have come here with only one goal in mind: to help our blind!'

'This is no way to show them our appreciation,' someone else chimed in.

'Furthermore,' said a third, 'you know as well as I that blind people don't use or need any electric light. It's therefore not only preposterous for you to charge them more than normal seeing people, it makes no sense!' Pushed against the wall, the employee reluctantly backed down. 'I'll take it up with the manager,' she said. And our bill was quickly reduced by two-thirds. I blessed our community for their vigilance.

★ ★ ★

Word of our school was spreading, bringing each day an increasing number of curious visitors. We had become a kind of local attraction. If visitors happened to stop in during class, Nordon, Anila, or Yishi would invite them in and demonstrate how our braille reading/writing machine functioned, or how our books could be read by the blind. During recess, it had become routine to see visitors watching and admiring how our children played ball games with their 'musical balls.'

The visitors were inevitably impressed, and in many cases profoundly moved. Many would come back bearing gifts, baskets of rice and flour. Some went so far as to hand us envelopes containing cash donations. I couldn't help remarking what an incredible contrast this was to our previous circumstances. I still had a bit of trouble getting used to this warm and supportive environment.

★ ★ ★

One morning, out of the blue, a wealthy Lhasa woman called our school. 'Would you accept a twelve-year-old boy in your program?'

'Absolutely,' I replied.

She had recently adopted a little blind boy off the street. We agreed to come right over to her house and interview the boy, whose name was Passang.

We found him standing in the courtyard in a defiant position, his hands covering his face.

'Hello, Passang, do you know who I am?' asked Nordon.

No answer. His silence lasted so long, in fact, that Nordon and I wondered whether he wasn't mute as well as blind.

Finally removing his hands from his face, Passang let go a flow of words. 'Of course I know who you are. You're the teacher at the school for the blind run by foreigners!'

'He knows all about your school!' the son of the house told us. 'The trouble with Passang is, he wants no part of any school. He much prefers begging on the Barkhor!'

'That's true,' the mother echoed. 'We've had quite an argument with him. He feels good out there on the street begging.'

'How do you manage to find your way about the city?' Nordon asked.

'I always walk where there are no cars. Whenever I need to cross the street, I ask someone to help me.'

'Where did you sleep this winter?' Nordon asked.

'In one of the market's stalls.'

'Didn't you freeze?'

'Oh, I wrapped myself in a big plastic sheet. I was fine.' Passang continued calmly, 'Of course, when my clothes were wet, I did get very cold. But I always managed to fall asleep, and once I slept, I wasn't cold anymore.' He smiled.

'I've often seen him,' someone I didn't know from the house interjected. 'I used to watch the police chase him. But he always outsmarted them. The police could never find him.'

'Ah, yes, I had stolen an apple. I remember that. The merchant wanted it back. I threw a stone at him,' Passang said.

'I saw other sighted kids in the street who always taunted him,' the son of the house added. 'They even took the money he had earned begging.'

'What about your *amala* and *pala?*' asked Nordon.

'My *pala?*' He answered, spitting on the floor. 'Saandreh!' (That son of a bitch!) 'When I was little, we lived far away, in the east of Tibet. One day, my father announced he was taking me on a trip to Lhasa. I was really happy to go away with my father — very few people in my village ever got to travel that far. And the idea of going to the capital was a big adventure. When we arrived in the city, all of a sudden things became clear to me. My father's only reason for bringing me there was to abandon me, because I was blind. He wanted to return home with a sighted child. He did find a little girl. Holding his new daughter's hands, with his other hand he took me over to a gang of beggars. When I resisted and ran back to him, he slapped me hard and yelled; 'You're on your own from now on! I don't want you in our family!'

I never saw him again. That's my *pala.*'

'What about your *amala?*'

'Yes, I do miss her. A little. But she is like him, a *saandreh*. Anyway, there is more food in the streets of Lhasa.'

'If you join us,' said Nordon softly, 'Anila will take care of you like a real mother. She'll clean your clothes, and show you how to wash yourself, brush your teeth, comb your hair.'

'No way!' Passang responded, 'I'd be too ashamed. All she needs is to give me some soap and point me in the direction of the well. I'll do the rest.'

'How about going to school? How do you feel about that?'

'I've never been to school. I like the Barkhor better.'

'In school, you'd learn Chinese.'

'Really?' he said. And he suddenly broke into fluent Chinese.

'Do you know how to count?'

'No.'

Nordon wasn't accepting defeat, not yet.

'How much is five plus five?'

'I don't know. I told you I've never been to school.'

'I give you five yuan, and the cook gives you another five. How many yuan do you have in your pocket?'

'Ten, of course!' he said, shrugging his shoulders.

'Someone gives you nine yuan, someone else gives you another forty-four. How many yuan do you now have?' I couldn't resist chiming in.

'Fifty-three! But no one ever gave me that kind of money!'

We were amazed.

'If you come to our school,' Nordon went on, 'you'll be the best in both Chinese and math. You'll be able to help the others.'

Passang clapped his hands: 'Really? You mean I'll be the best, and I'll be able to help the others?' he repeated to himself.

That seemed to do it. Clearly, no one in his short life had ever remotely suggested he could be good at anything. Our short conversation with him had given Passang a glimmer of possible dignity, and better things to come.

'He won't have any problem learning,' Nordon said on our way back. 'We'll have to see how the others take to him.'

Several days later, Passang arrived, carrying his few belongings, which consisted of the clothes he was wearing and a little recording machine — a gift from his adopted family.

His arrival created suspicion on the part of our little group of children, especially Meto, who was always ready to use her fists if necessary, and wasn't at all sure how to take this tough, uncouth street kid, who was so cocksure. One day, when Passang refused to lend her his recorder, I heard her shout, 'Anyway, who wants anything to do with a beggar!'

She tried rallying the other boys, particularly Gyendsen, to fight with him. No one reacted to her appeal, apparently preferring to insult him from afar.

Fed up, Passang one day stuffed his pockets with some cakes and flew the coop. It was Tendsin who noticed he was gone. Running up to us, he urged us to go after him. We didn't have far to go. In a nearby street, there was Passang, sitting on a stone, crying bitterly.

'Please come back!' Nordon pleaded. 'You'll be so much better off with us than in the street!'

'But I don't like the other children. And they don't like me. So how can I teach them anything?'

'Be patient,' Nordon said. 'They'll come around, you'll see.' Passang dried his tears and held out his hand, which Nordon took, and we brought him back home.

From that moment on, Passang became Tendsin's protégé, and Meto agreed to leave him be.

Because learning Tibetan braille seemed easy for Passang, I added European braille, and Nordon initiated him to Chinese braille writing. In less than two months, Passang had caught up with the whole school and was completely at ease with the other pupils.

I still had not found a replacement for Palden. Then one day a young man from Shigatse appeared out of nowhere at the school, offering his services. He wanted no salary, just a roof over his head and some food. We decided to try him out and have never regretted our decision.

Shigatse possessed the same wonderful attributes Nordon and Anila had: he was eager to work and learn. It took no time at all to teach him braille and orientation techniques for the blind.

Some of our neighbors were wary, warning us that this seemingly disinterested fellow might well be a spy, whose mandate was to check on us and make sure we weren't involved in any subversive activities.

'Spy or no spy,' said Paul, 'he's a great worker, potentially a great teacher, and he's nice to boot. Anyway, if he is a spy, what better way for us to have him expose us as harmless folks? It's fine with me.'

Jojo, as the children had named him, proved to be a dynamic and terrific house father. Aside from his regular teaching, he became our sports coach as well as the entertainment monitor. Gym was his new addition to our program. He also introduced soccer, and several other games.

Jojo also often took the children on picnics, which they always liked, as well as boat rides on a nearby lake, by the Potala. The children were always very excited and energized when they returned from those outings. After one of these trips I asked Gyendsen, why he was jumping up and down so. In his newly learned English he answered, 'I don't know. I am just sooo happy.'

There were also trips to the center of town, where Jojo taught the children how to navigate with the help of their canes. Gyendsen and Tendsin proved particularly agile, weaving in and around crowds in Lhasa's streets. They were so fast and adroit with the cane, Jojo often had trouble keeping up with them. The added bonus to that little exercise was that, for the first time, the Lhasa population was being introduced to little blind children moving about with a cane. Intrigued, passersby asked our children questions. For us, there was no better ambassador for our cause than Tendsin and Gyendsen, who always babbled joyfully at the drop of a question, explaining to whoever was listening all the wonderful things they were learning in school.

It was through that kind of word of mouth that little six-year-old Zidiggi and her family heard about us. Her grandmother brought her to us. At first she looked around, inspecting us carefully. She wasn't at all sure about our institution, and the more she looked, the more she shook her head. But her granddaughter asked impatiently, 'I know all about your school. When can I start?'

Zidiggi had been pampered by her family and acted a bit like a princess. In our school, she would no longer be the center of attention, and at first that concerned us. Not being able to do everything she set her mind to was a new experience for her. Still, she wanted to stay with us and seemed to enjoy her new environment.

One day, however, she fell down a flight of stairs and got up looking like a boxer after a rough fight — her nose all swollen. The other kids began calling her 'Big Nose.' That evening her grandmother promptly appeared however, not at all amused. She informed us she was taking Zidiggi out of the school. Immediately. The little girl insisted on calling her father — who was estranged from her mother — and pleaded with him to let her stay. So once again her grandmother was overruled.

★　★　★

News travels fast in Tibet. One day an old blind man who had heard about our school showed up. He had undertaken the long journey all the way from his hometown, 1,200 miles away, to ask if we would agree to take his three children, all of whom had been born blind. His wife was in the hospital with a heart condition, and he couldn't cope any longer. We were ready to accept his children, but had to have the governor's approval. And in Tibet, we explained to the old man, that kind of official paperwork could take us much as six months — which would bring us up to Christmas.

Four days later the phone rang. 'May I please come by?' It was the man with the three blind children.

'Of course,' we said, wondering what was the point of the visit.

An hour or two later he appeared at our door, his three blind children in tow: two thirteen-year-old twin boys, Dorje and Zampa, and their sister, Kila, one year older than the boys.

'But where are the documents?' asked Paul, incredulous and worried.

Bursting out laughing, the father proudly pulled out of his pocket the duly signed documents. How he had managed to get the necessary papers so quickly was a complete mystery to us all. And we never found out. But there they were, all three, ready to start school.

Many more such new candidates knocked at our door. Word continued to travel, and before we knew it, three more arrived: Yudon, eleven, brought to us by an ophthalmologist; Wugyan, seven, who had been living up to now in the street with his grandfather; and Ngudup, a shy little fellow who had traveled all the way from the foot of Mount Everest. We now had over a dozen children, all learning to navigate with a cane through the city, play sports, and read and write in three languages. Lhasa didn't quite know what to make of it.

30

In the fall of 1999, after the long rainy season, Paul and I felt it was time to let our extremely able Tibetan colleagues take charge of the school. The time had come for us to go back to Europe. It was imperative to find investors, to raise funds on a serious basis.

'What's going to happen to us when the big children leave?' asked Chila, worried.

'We'll just have to show everyone that we too can behave like older children!' replied Amala, laughing.

On the eve of our departure we organized a big party. All the children had asked to have a haircut for the occasion. Dolma came, and together with Yishi they went to work, shaving all the little heads, transforming our children into miniature monks.

'My grandmother will be pleased not to have to take me to the beauty parlor anymore,' Zidiggi exclaimed, after running her hands over her head.

'And tell your grandmother there won't be any more lice in your hair!'

As with our 'chrisse misse' celebration, a

great effervescence swept over the school. The cooks went into high gear. Mounds of various salads appeared in bowls, fragrant smells of cakes permeated the whole house, everyone was helping to stuff meat into vegetables for the preparation of fritters. Tendsin and Passang were scurrying about, helping move furniture, and decorating the place. 'We plan on dancing tonight. No tears allowed. Just good fun!' Amala announced.

'Today we are happy because they are still with us. Tomorrow, we'll be happy because they'll return to us soon,' she sang.

And the party began. Nordon gave a speech in her best English, wishing us bon voyage and great success: 'We will miss you, but never never worry. All children are good and hard work. Take care and come back soon!'

Little Sonam, who couldn't keep a tune but always wanted to sing, to the despair of one and all, banged on the table, shouting, 'All of you here! The famous Sonam Wangdu will sing his farewell song!' As he prepared to start, Meto rushed up to him in an effort to kill the project, but the others quickly surrounded her.

'Tonight everyone has the right to sing, even Sonam!' He sang for us, and his song was received with a big round of applause.

'Now it's Chila's turn!' And all in chorus: 'Chila! Chila!'

Flattered, Chila the performer got up, relishing the silence.

Amala had taught him to bow before singing, which he did. But not realizing he was standing close to a table, he banged his head. In the midst of general laughter that followed, charitable Amala brought a wet cloth, which she pressed on his forehead.

Overcoming his pain, Chila sang the best song he had ever sung to date, and his performance was judged a triumph.

Four of the oldest girls had prepared a ballet for us based on the story of the beautiful Yangdula, whose desire was to initiate her friends to the art of dancing. She was demonstrating that she could move each part of her body separately. After the feet dance came the neck dance, then the head dance. Mesmerized, the children got up and improvised their own dance for us. Before their dances degenerated into chaos, Nordon restored some semblance of order by performing a dance where the only sound we could hear was the movements of her silk blouse. The entire audience, blind and sighted, fell under the spell of her grace, charm, and talent.

A beautiful voice none of us had heard

before rose above the already general happy noise. It was Yishi, singing an old-fashioned Tibetan-style ballad evoking wide desert landscapes, a burning sun, and the mountains of Tibet. It sounded odd, even slightly scary, illustrating dust, drought, pain, and hopeless misery. Paul and I were very moved by her surprise ballad.

'You come, Mr. Paul. We need disco now!' shouted Amala.

We pulled out our CD player and put on our CDs. All the children, staff, and our guests got up and joined in a frenetic dance, yelling and stamping their feet until midnight, when we called a halt to the party.

'I always want to stay in school!' Gyendsen declared.

'We all do!' said Yudon. 'It's so much fun, and we learn so many new things all the time. We can dance and play and sing! Back home, we're always in everybody's way.'

It was a double-edged compliment. Paul and I were a little uneasy about the whole notion. What would they all do when it came time for them to return home? Our goal, of course, was not to alienate the children from their families. On the contrary, the idea had been for them to stay one, two years at most, in the school. In fact, our first children were almost ready to go home now.

'Don't you think it'll be more fun for you to be able to go to school with your brothers and sisters, and your friends back home?'

'Maybe,' Gyendsen said. 'But later I want to come back here and be like Jojo, take care of the children, be a teacher/coach/house father.'

'I want to become a doctor!' Meto announced.

This went on for quite a while. Some voiced the desire to become a cook, a tailor, a driver of a jeep, a dancer. Chila's choice was to become a car.

★ ★ ★

'It'll be a nice change for us to take a warm shower again, and eat a real square meal,' Paul mused. 'But I have to confess I'll miss this country and the children so much!'

It was late as we walked through the Barkhor and arrived back at the Banak Shol. Lhasa, we had come to realize, with its broken-down roads, its impossible old houses, the strong perfumed fragrances the temples exuded (along with its dreadful other smells), its narrow streets, had become our second home by now.

The next morning, we said good-bye to everyone. The children were sitting on top of our suitcases, sniffling. Even Nordon seemed anguished. 'Are you afraid of taking responsibility for the school for a few months?' we asked.

'Not at all. What concerns me is whether the authorities will renew your reentry visas and your working permits.' But she added quickly, 'Don't worry! If worse comes to worst, I'll run the school!'

Under normal circumstances, Paul and I travel with our backpacks. But a great many people had loaded us up with gifts for our respective families, and we had to travel more encumbered than usual. Amala gave us a big basket of food for the journey, and Jojo asked us to kindly carry an enormous case to a friend in Kathmandu.

'Lucky we're not traveling during the rainy season,' Paul said. 'We would never make it with all this luggage!'

It was time for our final good-byes. We found ourselves at the center of a tragicomic scene: standing by the jeep that was to take us across, we were surrounded by fourteen sobbing children, not to mention the adults, all trying to console one another. To add to the chaos, a number of neighbors had also gathered. We must have been quite a spectacle. Neither taxis nor buses could get through, so all began madly honking their horns. We had created a real traffic jam.

Tsering, our trusty driver, was also growing impatient, honking his horn as well and gunning the motor. Winding our way through the teary crowd, we hopped into the car, and off Tsering drove.

Both Paul and I left with a heavy heart; it was as if we were leaving part of us behind.

It took only two days to arrive at the Nepalese border this time. Our first stop was in a village ten thousand feet above sea level, called Nyalam. It was quite a contrast coming from the previous scenery, which was rather like a lunar landscape. At that altitude, it's very cold, but Paul and I took a walk nonetheless in this startling landscape of mountains topped with white caps.

As soon as we got to the other side of the mountain, we found ourselves suddenly in the midst of flowers and rich, green forests through which rushing rivers ran. I leaned out of the car window, the better to take in this drastic change. Gone were the glacial wind, dust, and sand. The air was growing progressively more humid, and I could breathe deeply again.

We arrived at the border town of Zhangmu after two hours of narrow winding roads. It had become much hotter, and a strong smell of manure filled the air. Zhangmu was always a shock for us. We felt we had suddenly landed on a planet we didn't particularly care to be on. This sinister town had a way of making us anticipate our friend's welcome in Nepal, and further, our return to Europe.

This time, the passport control office was open and allowed Tsering to drive us across to the border. There we bid him good-bye, loaded our luggage as best we could on our backs, and marched off to the Friendship Bridge, where a guard examined our papers. Taking a look at Jojo's oversize crate, the soldier asked, 'What's this?'

Feeling immediately in danger, I tried hard to hide my anxiety, a frozen smile fixed on my lips. How stupid, how naive we had been! I thought. What if that crate contained forbidden documents, contraband? And who was Jojo, anyway? We hadn't really properly checked him out, had we? If there were forbidden things inside, we were finished! We could never return to Tibet. This soldier had been warned of our arrival, I was convinced, and was ready to arrest us. Meanwhile Paul was struggling to open the case. When it finally opened, he and the guard leaned over and peered inside, to discover that it contained some silk, a few wooden bowls, and a few other souvenirs for Jojo's family in Kathmandu. The guard, with the trace of a smile, waved us across into Nepal.

EPILOGUE

May 2002

After a several-month-long fund-raising stay in Europe, we flew back to Nepal early in 2000 with the intention of traveling to Lhasa by land. However, as had happened once before, the promised entry papers were still being processed, and we had to spend four weeks in Kathmandu, frustrated and increasingly worried. We called Nordon every two days: 'The papers were not ready yet! Perhaps next week. Perhaps even later!'

★   ★   ★

We compared our wait-and-see-stay in Kathmandu to being enclosed in a starting gate that was too small. We were like nervous racehorses, waiting for the starting signal. What were the reasons for the interminable delay this time? Were we no longer wanted? Was something going on behind the scenes of which we had no clue? We could never get used to Tibetan bureaucracy.

After four long weeks, our papers finally

came through. Three days later we landed at the Lhasa airport, where we were greeted by a beaming Nordon. She had some excellent news: the training center for the blind of Tibet — our school — was no longer just tolerated, it was officially accepted by the Tibetan government! In cooperation with our new partner, the Tibetan Disabled Persons Federation (TDPF), we could finally put our plans into action.

* * *

Two years after the start, thanks to worldwide support, we can now consider our school for the blind a major achievement. A new building, built by Paul, which we annexed to the old school building, is dedicated to a braille book press, where we print Tibetan, Chinese, and English schoolbooks; more classrooms and more dormitories for the students have been added, as well as a medical massage center, and for the first time in years, a small but comfortable temporary home for Paul and me.

Thanks to several worldwide media reports, the project has become well known: schools, clubs, private donors, and organizations have helped us turn a small initiative into a firm and secure enterprise.

At the end of 1998 the Kölner EP-Stiftung, a new German foundation for developing aid projects, put their own bank account at our disposal to collect donations for our project. We are particularly thankful to the small group of Bank employees, and above all to its founder, Stefan Dresbach.

Also toward the end of 1998, Frans van Bennekom, now deceased, set up the foundation Doel voor Ogen (a Goal for/before Eyes) in Amsterdam. Since then this dedicated group has taken care of our Dutch patrons, and constantly campaigned for new sponsors.

In May 1999 the Förderkreis Blindzentrum Tibet e.V. was founded in Morenhoven near Bonn. It took over the management of the sponsors of the EP-Stiftung and became a reliable pillar for our work in Germany. It is the center of our work in Europe.

Twenty-seven students, ranging in age from four to twenty-two, are now being trained, in different ways, for a self-determined life in Tibetan society. Our school continues to prepare students to be integrated in regular schools. Our mission is also setting up a training site in which blind youth and blind grown-ups are trained according to their age and capabilities for various jobs. In this program we concentrate on activities that are needed in Tibet, considering the abilities and possibilities of each individual blind student.

Since November 2000 two blind teachers have already successfully trained some of the students to become medical masseurs and physiotherapists. (In China, this profession has been reserved for the blind and the deaf.) There is an urgent need for masseurs in the Tibetan highlands because of a peculiar but widespread disease, the cause of which has not yet been determined. The victims of this disease develop overly large joints and become increasingly handicapped as they grow older. Massages and physiotherapeutic treatment can help these people move again without pain. The masseurs we train will all have guaranteed jobs.

Four of our students have been taught by a blind musician how to sing professionally and play musical instruments. Entertainment at the Nangma — a Tibetan disco of sorts — is much loved, and also guarantees sustenance as well as prestige.

Other possible professions for the blind in Tibet are cattle rancher or tiller. Farmers and nomads in particular who live in remote altitudes often suffer from eye diseases that lead to total blindness. With appropriate techniques, methods, and therapy, these people are being reintegrated into their old jobs. To this end, a farm is being built outside Lhasa. Farmers or ranchers who became blind as grownups can relearn how to deal with plants and animals. We created another avenue of revenue for the blind: they are taught how to make cheese — not only the traditional Tibetan dry cheese, so hard we often worry about our teeth. We hired a Swiss cheesemaker to teach us how to manufacture cheese, and thanks to him, cheese that is more attractive to Western palates will be made commercially available. A mozzarella we'll call Lhasarella, perhaps? Or even a Tibet Brie? We are working in this direction, which will become an additional source of income for the blind.

The past two years were not as easy as we had hoped. Again there were many unexpected obstacles and regressions, which meant that the construction of the rehabilitation center took longer than we had hoped. Paul and I plan to remain in Lhasa for another year and a half, after which we plan to hand over the reins to our Tibetan colleagues, our local counterparts. And then?

We have founded an organization that we call Braille without Borders. Our plan is to travel from country to country, from continent to continent, and wherever there's need set up small braille presses and training centers for the blind. These are to become 'help for self-help' projects, in which the blind will be involved first and foremost as cofounders and managers. Once things are up and functioning, we will, once again, sadly have to say good-bye to the projects we have built.

As for our children in Lhasa, it will not be easy for us to part from them. We have a huge emotional investment there. But we must take our path away from Tibet and found other such centers throughout the world. This said, the bonds formed in Lhasa will make it extremely difficult to leave. Like parents, we will always wonder about our charges, and whether things are going well in Lhasa. When we went back to Europe in 1999, the constantly encouraging letters from Nordon reassured us that the children were in good hands and the project going forward, almost standing on its own two feet. And of that we are immensely proud.

Letters from Nordon

November 1999

Dear Sabriye and Paul:

How are both of you? I am very missing you. All the things going very well, please

351

do not worry. Our students are hard work and all the staff are very good in their work, too.

These days Norbu is little bit sick, he got a cold, but not worry. He is fine. Dorje had little sick with a cold. I think these days so cold. We took him to the hospital, he is better now. So please do not worry.

We are very well. But Ngudup has infection with his ears. Jampa, he got high fever and cold. Housemother and housefather are very care for to them, every day they took them to the hospital, get injection and they looks better than before.

Meto fall down in faint, doctor do not know what wrong with her. Now she is very good and happy. Everything goes very well, do not worry.

December 1999

Dear Sabriye and Paul:

School is near vacation, so I already contact the family. We can see later, how to send the children. But do not worry with them, I can do all the thing.

The mother of Tendsin, she come here, she want take Tendsin back home earlier. So I give 20 Yuan to him. When he leave he was cry and cry. Other students, they never say they want go home. They like study and enjoying their life.

January 2000

These day the weather is dry and so cold in the morning. The winter is come very fast in this year. All the students were sent. They were very sad when they leaving. They are so sweet. All the thing going very well, do not worry about us.

February 2000

It is near the New Year, so we are little bit busy. Also I think our project will be very good and successful in this new year. I am very missing you and Paul. I will do my best. Here my mother wish you good luck and happy.

March 2000

From yesterday we begin the class. All the students are arrived. They are very happy. Also there is new student, he is introduced by Dolma. His name is Gyumi, seven years old.

Today is very noisy in our school,

because all the students are talking and singing. They talk about New Year, their family and school. They say: 'I am the first student who come back to school. I am the second student . . . ' They are very lovely. Also they are having lesson now. All the thing goes very well, don't worry about the students.

Yesterday all the staff and students cleaned all the garden and classroom. So we have a very nice school and garden. All the students are studying and playing. They say we make it very clean and Paul and Sabriye will very happy.

The children are missing you so much, all the time they say when do you come back?

Did you get my mail with book-keeping?

Every thing goes very well, so do not worry about us.

You are happy and I BIG happy.

We do hope that you have enjoyed reading this large print book.

Did you know that all of our titles are available for purchase?

We publish a wide range of high quality large print books including:
Romances, Mysteries, Classics
General Fiction
Non Fiction and Westerns

Special interest titles available in large print are:
The Little Oxford Dictionary
Music Book
Song Book
Hymn Book
Service Book

Also available from us courtesy of Oxford University Press:
Young Readers' Dictionary
(large print edition)
Young Readers' Thesaurus
(large print edition)

For further information or a free brochure, please contact us at:
Ulverscroft Large Print Books Ltd.,
The Green, Bradgate Road, Anstey,
Leicester, LE7 7FU, England.
Tel: (00 44) 0116 236 4325
Fax: (00 44) 0116 234 0205

Other titles published by
The House of Ulverscroft:

ONLY A MOTHER COULD LOVE HIM

Ben Polis

Ben Polis attended six different schools, served approximately 5,000 detentions, and drove his entire family into counselling. But with a combination of self-taught concentration techniques and sheer determination, he made it through the education system to university. This is his triumphant story — and a remarkable look inside the mind of a person with ADHD — Attention Deficit Hyperactive Disorder. Ben describes what it's like to feel those constant inexplicable impulses, to get all that medication, to desperately want to be 'normal'. His frank and often funny account will enlighten every parent who's ever despaired of their seemingly uncontrollable child.